HUBERT'S WIFE

A Story for You

MINNIE MARY LEE

Hubert's Wife

Minnie Mary Lee

© 1st World Library, 2007
PO Box 2211
Fairfield, IA 52556
www.1stworldlibrary.com
First Edition

LCCN: 2007934194

Softcover ISBN: 978-1-4218-9663-2
Hardcover ISBN: 978-1-4218-9763-9
eBook ISBN: 978-1-4218-9563-5

Purchase *"Hubert's Wife"*
as a traditional bound book at:
www.1stWorldLibrary.com/purchase.asp?ISBN=978-1-4218-9663-2

1st World Library is a literary, educational organization
dedicated to:

- Creating a free internet library of downloadable ebooks

- Hosting writing competitions and offering book publishing
scholarships.

Interested in more 1st World Library books? contact:
literacy@1stworldlibrary.com
Check us out at: www.1stworldlibrary.com

1ˢᵗ World Library Literary Society

Giving Back to the World

"If you want to work on the core problem, it's early school literacy."

- James Barksdale, former CEO of Netscape

"No skill is more crucial to the future of a child, or to a democratic and prosperous society, than literacy."

- Los Angeles Times

"Literacy... means far more than learning how to read and write... The aim is to transmit... knowledge and promote social participation."

- UNESCO

"Literacy is not a luxury, it is a right and a responsibility. If our world is to meet the challenges of the twenty-first century we must harness the energy and creativity of all our citizens."

- President Bill Clinton

"Parents should be encouraged to read to their children, and teachers should be equipped with all available techniques for teaching literacy, so the varying needs and capacities of individual kids can be taken into account."

- Hugh Mackay

"There is a way which seemeth just to a man, but the end thereof leadeth unto death."

—Prov. xlv, 12.

CONTENTS

CHAPTER I

A BLACK CONFERENCE

It was the night after the funeral. Ellice Lisle, the loving wife, devoted mother, kind mistress, and generous friend, had been laid away to rest; over her pulseless bosom had been thrown the red earth of her adopted Virginia, and, mingled with its mocking freshness, was the bitter rain of tears from the eyes of all who had known the lowly sleeper. Even Nature joined the general weeping; for, though the early morning had been bright and beautiful, ere the mourners' feet had left the new-made grave, the skies had lowered, and a gentle rain descended.

"*You* have pity upon me, O Heaven, and you weep for me, O earth," had exclaimed Duncan Stuart Lisle, as, leading his little Hubert by the hand, he turned away from his lost Ellice.

As night deepened, the rain increased, and the darkness became intense. The house-servants, timid and superstitious, had all congregated in Aunt Amy's cabin. Amidst their grief, sincere and profound, was yet a subject of indignation, which acted as a sort of safety-valve to their over-much sorrowing.

"A nice, pretty piece of impudence it was, to be sure, when she hadn't been in the house for five year, to 'trude herself the minute Miss Ellice's breath had left her precious body, the poor dear!" ejaculated Chloe, the cook, who was intensely black, and fat to immensity.

"Much as ever Massa Duncan 'peared to notice her, not'standing she make herself so 'ficious," said Amy, who looked more the Indian than African.

"He never set eyes on her but once," said young China, the favorite housemaid, whose dialect and manners were superior to those of the other servants, "only just once, and that was when she looked at him so long and fierce-like he couldn't actually keep his eyes down."

"I see it my own self," added Chloe, whose small orbs were almost buried beneath overhanging cliffs of brow and uprising mountains of cheek, "and I'll tell you what I tinks: I tinks just den and dere, dat if we's meet de ole one hisself he wouldn't hab no eyes, cause Misses Rusha Rush jes done gone an' stole 'em."

This dark reference caused a closer grouping of the sable dames and damsels. Trembling hands drew small plaid shawls closer about the shoulders, while one bolder than the rest cast a huge pine-knot upon the glowing coals.

Amy was first to break the brief silence.

"Mighty pity Jude Rush ever fell off 'Big Thunderbolt' and broke his slim neck! But Massa Duncan knew nuf once to let Miss Rusha 'lone; he's not gwine to be 'veigled by none o' her hilofical airs—you may 'pend on dat; 'specially when he's had dat sweet saint all to hisself now dese so many year—no, neber."

And Amy reiterated this over and over, as if to kill the secret thought which haunted her against her will.

"She persume to come here and order you dis way an' I dat way, an' all us all 'round ebry which way—oo—but I gived her a piece o' my mind," spake Margery, the weaver, very irate.

"Umph! I never seed ye speak to her," said Amy, doubtingly.

"Not wid my tongue, mind ye. I knows better den dat. But I jes spit fire at her out of my eyes."

"Fire neber burn Miss Rusha; she too ugly for dat. S'pose fire burn de ole Nick? Den he be done dead and gone, which ain't so; derefore nuthin' ever fall Miss Rusha; she never sick, nor die, nor drown, nor burn up. Miss Ellice she sick, she die, 'cause she be an angel; she go home to glory; but Miss Rusha she live, jes to trouble white folks, jes to torment niggers."

Wrathful Amy, as she said this, glanced triumphantly at Margery, who was about to speak, when Chloe took the floor, figuratively.

"Tank de Lord, we ain't de niggers what she's got to torment; and she needn't be setting her cap for our own good Massa Duncan; she may jes hang up high her fiddle on de willows o' Bab'lon; she sit down an' weep on de streams; she neber hab good Massa Duncan; neber while de trees on Kennons grow and de stars 'bove Kennons shine."

Kennons was the name of the Lisle plantation.

"She'd like to jine the two plantations. One is too little for her to rule. She's allus wanted our south 'bacco patch. Her hundred niggers and Massa's hundred would make a crew. O, she's a shrewd one; she sees further than her nose. She'd make my shettle fly fast as Aunt Kizzie's."

"Somebody ought to make your shuttle fly faster than is its habit, Margery," returned China, usually quiet and gentle. "But what if you are all mistaken, and Mistress Rush has no idea of making a rush upon Kennons and our good master."

"O, you poor innocent," quoth Chloe and Amy at the same time. "Haven't we eyes? What's they for if not to see with? They ain't in the backs of our heads neither. We've got ears too; we don't hear with our elbows. What for did she bring nice things and pretties for Hubert? and what for did she take such a wonderful interest in de poor baby? Bress us, is de baby wake or sleep, or what is come of it? We's all forgettin' de dear precious objec. Sakes alive, an' its nearly smuddered in its soft blankets, worked so beau'fully wid its own moder's hand."

A sleeping-powder, administered to the three days' old infant had, for a time, quieted its incessant cries. This sudden mention brought every dark face to bend low over the cradle, which Bessie, the nurse, had brought hither from the house, that she might share the gossip of her companions.

Worn out with weeping and watching, Bessie lay prone and sleeping upon the floor at the cradle's side. Satisfied that the baby still breathed, Chloe, Amy, Margery, China and Dinah settled back into their seats, like so many crows upon a branch.

Dinah, the last-named, had been thus far fast asleep; and provoked with herself that she had lost a share of the gossip, she gave Bessie a vigorous push with her foot as she passed her, not through charity, nor yet through malice, but through a sudden spasm of ill-nature.

Bessie gave a groan and sat up. She gazed around wildly—

slowly comprehended the scene, the present, the past, and, with another groan, flung herself upon the floor again.

"You ought to be ashamed of yourself, Dinah, to disturb Bessie in that way," said China, between whom and Bessie was a warm friendship. "She has cried so, and broken her heart."

"She needn't be in people's way, then—who's going 'round Robinhood's barn for sake o' likes o' her?" said Dinah, complainingly.

"Shut your mouth, black Dinah," cried Amy authoritatively. "Ye's a pretty one to knock around a sleepin' nigger. You's been asleep yourself the last hour. S'pose we'd all been like you—you'd been kicked into a heap—but we ain't—and you never *did* have a drop o' human kindness."

"O, go 'way wid your quarreling. Dinah is jis like a firebran'; let her 'lone. What she got to do wid dis subjec-matter in han', I like a-know?" queried Aunt Chloe, swaying up to the mantle, filling her pipe with tobacco, and adding thereto the smallest glowing coal upon the hearth. Meantime, while she is preparing for a smoke, her companions have taken from their pockets, each a tin snuff-box and a mop, which mop consists of a small twig, chewed at the end into threads or fibers. This mop, wet with saliva, is thrust into the box of Scotch snuff, thence thrust into the mouth, and worked around upon the teeth much to the delight and constant spitting of the performer. This operation, so prevalent both among white and black women of the South, is called "*dipping* snuff."

Having followed our sable friends from grief to indignation, and from indignation to the charming amusement of snuff-dipping, we will enter the house and make acquaintance with its master.

CHAPTER II

THE MASTER'S CONFERENCE WITH HIMSELF

It was late in September, and chilly for the season. A bright fire glowed upon the hearth in the "lady's chamber" at Kennons. Red curtains shaded the windows, and drooped in folds to the floor. Roses and green leaves seemed springing up out of the carpet to meet the light and warmth that radiated from the small semicircle behind the glittering fender. A bed hung with white curtains, a dressing bureau, with its fancy pincushion, and numerous cut-glass bottles of perfumery, a lounge covered with bright patchwork, and furnished with log-cabin cushions, easy-chairs and ottomans, together with the workstand and its inseparable little basket filled with every indispensable for needlework—all, all bore the trace of woman's hand.

For nine years this had been the loved family-room of Duncan and Ellice Lisle.

Now, Ellice was forever gone. Her foot had passed the threshold, to come in, to go out, no more. Her canary hung in the window; how could he sing on the morrow, missing *her* accustomed voice? Her picture hung over the mantle, looking down with the old-time brightness upon the the solitary figures beforefire—Duncan and his child.

Hubert, the son, in his eighth year, sitting clasped in his father's arms, had pierced anew that tortured heart by asking questions about his mother and the mystery of death, which no human mind can answer. The child was in a vortex of wonder, grief and speculation. It was the first great lesson of his life, and he would learn it well, the more that it was so severe and incomprehensible. But sleep and fatigue overcame Hubert at length. The light from the fire no more danced with his shifting curls, but settled down in a steady golden glow over the mass that mingled its yellow-brown with the black beard of the stricken man. For the father would not lay away his sleeping child. He held him close, as the something, the all that was left to him of his lost love. His head drooped low and his lips rested in a long embrace of the child's soft wealth of hair.

Mayhap some watching spirit took pity upon the man bereaved; for while he gazed into the fire, the heavy pressure of the present yielded to a half-conscious memory of the past, and a dream-like reverie brightened and darkened, flickered and burned in and out with the red of the flame, and the white of the ashes.

Duncan Lisle was a boy again. With two little brothers and a half-dozen black child-retainers, he hunted in the woods of Kennons, sailed boats on the red waters of the Roanoke, rode break-neck races over the old fields, despising fences high, and ditches deep, and vigorously sought specimens of uncouth, out-of-the-way beast, bird and insect. He studied mathematics and classics, played pranks upon one tutor, and did loving reverence to another. He planted flowers upon his own mother's grave, and filled the vases of his stepmother with her own favorite lilacs and roses. He made houses, carriages, swings, sets of furniture, and all sorts of constructions for his half-sister Della, who was his junior by ten years at least.

He edified, not to say terrified, the dusky crowd of juveniles with jack-o'-lanterns, impromptu giants and brigands, false faces, fire crackers, ventriloquism and sleight-of-hand performances.

With a decided propensity for fun and mischief, there was also in his disposition as evident a proclivity to seriousness and earnestness. If it gave him delight to play off upon a stranger the joke of "bagging the game," he enjoyed with equal ardor the correct rendering of a difficult translation, or the solution of an intricate problem.

If sometimes he annoyed with his untimely jest, he always won by his manly openness and uniform kindliness of nature. He cherished love for all that was around him, both animate and lifeless. Soul and Nature therefore rendered back to him their meed of harmonious sympathy.

Duncan was scarcely seventeen when the Plague swept over Kennons. That mysterious blight, rising in the orient, traveling darkly and surely unto the remotest West, laid its blackened hand upon the fair House of Kennons.

Cholera! fearful by name and by nature, it was not so strange that thy skeleton fingers should clutch at the myriad-headed city, situate by river and by sea, but thou wert insatiable! Proud dwellings and lowly cots in green fields and midst waving woods thou didst not spare; for thy victim, the human form, was there.

In the middle of August, the skies shone over Kennons happy and fair. Some cousins came down from the city seeking safety—bringing, alas, suffering and death!

In one little month, how fearful a change!

Duncan Lisle, sitting before the fire on this sad rainy evening, after the lapse of twenty years, shudders as he recalls the blackened pall that seemed spread over earth and air.

Strange to say, the disease prevailed least amongst the frightened servants.

The hundred were perhaps decimated.

In the house only Duncan and his half-sister Della survived; they in fact escaped the contagion. The father, a strong, healthy man, struggled bravely with the fierce attack; he even rallied, until there was good hope of his recovery. But a sudden relapse bore him swiftly beyond mortal remedy. Duncan, in his reverie, closes his eyes, to shut out the fearful memory. He glides over his college years and his sister's course at school. He sees Jerusha Thornton in her youth and pride and beauty. She waves off the many suitors in her train, only to smile winsomely at the young master of Kennons. Her estate is equal to, and adjoins his own. He has known her from her childhood—he loves no other—and still he loves not her. He revolves the reason of this in his own mind. She has beauty, wealth, accomplishments. He gives no credence to rumors of her cruelty to servants, though aware of her haughtiness to all, and her disdain to inferiors. The high favor which she showed to him would be welcomed with joy by at least a half-dozen of his acquaintance. But this, her manifest preference, did not please Duncan Lisle— there might be no accounting for it, but it was a fact.

What was to be done? Kennons needed sadly a woman at its head. Its master had come to be nearly twenty-eight, and not married yet!

The servants were in a state of terrified suspense, lest he

should bring Miss Rusha as their mistress. They wished their master to marry—they would dance for joy—but it must be some other young lady than the heiress of Thornton Hall.

Delia had been to a Northern school nearly five years; she would soon be eighteen, and was about to graduate.

As very young girls, Della and Rusha had known each other. For many years, however, having been at different schools they had rarely met.

Duncan held a faint impression that his half-sister had never been at all partial to this near neighbor of his. She was coming home so soon, he had such confidence in her judgment and womanly intuitions, he would await her coming, and see if she could divine why it was that while he *would* be attracted to Rusha Thornton he could not.

Besides, Della was not returning home alone. Ellice Linwood had been for five years her most intimate chosen friend, and room-mate. Ellice was the only child of a widowed Presbyterian clergyman. Her father had spent all he had to bestow upon her, in her education. This being thorough and complete, in the way such terms are used, she was henceforth to support herself by teaching.

In order to avoid a deplorable separation, these two young friends had put their wits together, and lo, the result! Through Della's good brother Duncan, a situation had been secured for Ellice in the family of Col. Anderson, not over six miles from Kennons. They would speedily become excellent equestrians, these friends, and annihilate the narrow space every day in the year.

CHAPTER III

AN INTERRUPTION TO DUNCAN'S REVERIE

Duncan Lisle, still gazing vacantly into the varying flames, performed anew the journey, not from Kennons to Troy on the Hudson, but from the latter city, via New York, back to his Virginian plantation. His sister and Ellice Linwood were his companions, for it had been arranged that, though Ellice's session of school was not to commence for a couple of months, yet she should thus early undertake the journey for sake of the company; and Della's home was to be hers also in the intervening time.

Della and Ellice! They flitted hither and thither before Duncan's mental vision, as they had on that memorable journey. Just free from the irksome restraints of the school-room, full of joyous anticipations, they gave way to that girlish gayety, and that unbounded enthusiasm, which a thorough sense of happiness and enjoyment cannot fail to inspire. Life was before them beautiful, glorious, and without end! This was only nine years ago—and now!

As we look through Duncan's eyes, we see that Della was the taller and more graceful of the two. Her hair and complexion were rather dark than fair; long, dark eyelashes shaded eyes deep blue, dreamy and wondrous in expression. We never mind much a nose, unless it be ugly to a deformity, or a model for the sculptor. An Angelo would have thrilled at sight of Della's nose, and straightway wrought it into immortality, *alto relievo*. Her mouth and chin were as lovely and divinely rounded as any Madonna's. The shape of her head was superb; and she wore her hair, which was truly a glory in itself, somewhat like a crown, which left her finely curved ear liberty to show itself and to hear everything that was going on. Many would have rhapsodised over her lithe, slender form. Not we. More admirable that faithful approach to those olden models of the human form that exist in artists' studios and adorn grand rooms of princely connoisseurs.

Nature is everywhere lovely. Had the ancient Greeks chiselled but the wasp waists of our modern belles, their hideous works would have sunk into oblivion in as little time as our self-made martyrs drop into early graves.

Not saying that Della Lisle, whose waist you could *not* "span with your two hands," had foolishly contributed to make less its natural size, but it was painfully suggestive of weakened lungs and an early translation.

Ellice, on the contrary, possessed a low, plump figure, all curve and dimple, with no appearance of angularity or stiffness. She had a fair, round face, cheeks in which roses came and went, laughing blue eyes, a wide, low brow, auburn curls, nose not *retrousse*, but the least bit inclined that way, white teeth, somewhat large, but pretty, that really *did* look like pearls between such cherry-red lips.

You might stand in respect and admiration before the dignified and intellectual Della Lisle; but Ellice Linwood you would take to your heart. If you were gay, she would laugh with you; if serious, she would become pensive; if sick, she would soothe and comfort you.

She was the most unselfish creature in existence. Self-denial ceased to become such to her; her happiness was in yours alone.

All things about the plantation brightened in presence of these two young maidens. Old servants grew more youthful, the young wiser and happier, and all, from black to brown, from young to old, as they looked upon the bright face of the northern stranger, turned dreamer and prophet. And this is what they dreamed and wished and foretold: that Master Duncan would make Ellice his wife and keep her forever.

And Duncan? Well, while such a spirit of prophecy reigned all around him, it is not to be supposed that it fell not on him also. He thought no more of seeking from his wise sister the solution of his antipathy to Miss Thornton. There was no room in his mind now for aught outside his home.

In three weeks he asked Ellice to be his wife. The same day he dispatched a letter to the Principal of the Troy Ladies' Seminary, soliciting a teacher for Colonel Anderson; another message, also, to the father of his affianced, begging him to come down at once and perform the marriage ceremony for his daughter.

This was doing up business very expeditiously. Of course it was soon noised near and far, that great quantities of snow-white cake were being made at Kennons kitchen. Servants would talk; little pitchers had ears, and birds carried news.

Miss Thornton went in state to call upon the strangers. She saw at a glance how matters stood, or were going to stand. She could have torn out Ellice's happy heart. As it was, she bowed to all haughtily as a queen, casting her last contemptuous glance at Miss Linwood's face.

Miss Thornton ordered to be driven rapidly homeward; and, as she was whirled along, her thoughts, in a swifter whirl, she meditated and resolved.

Before the bewildered clergyman could make his way down from the North, before the goddess of Rumor herself had even suspected such a thing, Miss Thornton's whole retinue of suitors, and the people at large were electrified by the astounding intelligence that Mr. Harris, from Flat Rock, had been summoned to Thornton Hall to unite in marriage its beautiful mistress, Miss Jerusha Thornton, to Doctor Jude Rush!

Dr. Jude Rush had the year previously emigrated to Mecklenburg county from the State of Maine. There was about him nothing so extraordinary as to require particular description. He was an ordinary country doctor, about thirty in years, had sandy hair, was sandy complexioned, and wore sandy clothes. This is not much to our taste, but then we did not marry him. We will assert, however, that had we been Madam Jerusha Thornton Rush, our first business would have been to engage him a black suit at the tailor's; but not a bottle of hair dye. We believe in adhering to nature, though insisting that nature can be much assisted, particularly in the matter of dress.

Duncan Lisle had naught for which to reproach himself. He had never made love to Miss Thornton, or given her reason for believing himself otherwise than indifferent. It had, however, been to him a source of uneasiness, this very knowledge of her unmistakable partiality for him. Of this he was quite relieved at news of her marriage, which news he received, with a bountiful supply of bridal cake, as soon as possible after the ceremony. He chewed his cake and sweet fancies of Ellice together. A week later, Mrs. Rush threw *his* wedding cake to the dogs, her own *bitter* fancies being sufficient for her to consume.

Faithful memory is on a race to-night, and she hurries Duncan Lisle from the beautiful picture of Ellice, his bride, over ground of a year or two, to that other picture, no less dear, that of Ellice, the mother of his child. The rose has paled a little in her cheek, but the love-light is in her eye; and can he ever, ever forget how, though he never called himself a Christian, his heart almost burst with thanksgiving to God when he clasped in his arms his world, his all—wife and child!

Three years from the other wedding, and another takes place at Kennons. Philip St. Leger has finished his course at Princeton, and come to take away his long-promised bride. The first wedding had been altogether joyous; this second was saddened and sorrowful. Della had become the wife of a missionary, and was to go at once to New York, taking ship thence to Turkey.

The cruel separation had come then at length to the tried and true friends; it might, nay, probably would, be forever in this world.

In the light of memory, Duncan beholds his sister for the last time. She is very dear to him, one only more dear. He turns to comfort Ellice; but Ellice, brave, heroic, crushes down her grief to comfort him.

With Della gone, the wife appears alone in the succeeding years. Alone, but ever bright and shining, whether amid her ebony domestics, or enthroned as wife and mother. Patient, cheerful, wise, and kind.

O, Ellice Lisle! model of all womanly virtues! Shall a Cady Stanton preach to such as thou? How wide with wonder and dismay would open those frank blue eyes at windy declamations about woman's rights, woman's freedom, and man's tyranny.

Woman voluntarily assumes the *chains* of matrimony. Be they of iron or of silk, the good wife discovereth not; for it is only in an unholy struggle that they bind and fetter.

Memory was hurrying Duncan Lisle apace to-night; scenes in the last few years shifted with surprising rapidity; everywhere Ellice was the centre-piece, her fair, pleasant face beaming from its framework of brown curls, that were almost ever in perpetual motion from the frequent toss of the busy little head.

But memory, though faithful, was pitiful, and kept presenting, one after another, undarkened pictures, full of glow and sunshine; she had not come down to the last three days of suspense and pain, of agony and desolation. Ere that cruel curtain of gloom should shut from the dreamer's eye his pleasant fancies, and with them the dying flames, the loud barking of dogs, soon succeeded by hurried steps and voices, aroused the half-conscious master of Kennons to the stern reality of the present moment.

CHAPTER IV

PHILIP ST. LEGER

Duncan Lisle, at once thoroughly aroused, laid his sleeping child upon the lounge, and then hastily opening the door, which led upon the veranda, encountered the bronzed face and flashing eyes of his brother-inlaw, Philip St. Leger. Now this gentleman from Turkey was not a ghost, nor had he rained down. A staunch ship had brought him from Constantinople to New York; a week he had spent with his friends at Troy; the lightning express, then so-called, from the latter city to Richmond; thence a stage had set him down at Flat-Rock; here, public conveyance went no farther. The best and only means of transportation was on horseback. The roads were in too wretched a condition for the "Bald Eagle's" one rickety carriage to attempt to plough through.

The returned missionary, almost distracted with care and fatigue, made a virtue of necessity. With black Sam as guide, he set off amid the rain and darkness for Kennons.

"It were better," he said, mentally, "that I should myself remain until the morning; but having come so far, so near, I should be on thorns; I must go."

Philip St. Leger was not a Virginian by birth. He was a

native of the city at whose distinguished school Della Lisle had graduated. Only on the day of graduation and at the time of her marriage had the brother and husband of Della met.

It was a sad meeting now, on this dreary night. These men, still in the flush of manhood, clasped hands, and looked into each others' eyes, with a despairing, inquiring eagerness.

Their chill fingers were scarce unlocked when Duncan asked:

"And did you come alone?"

"I brought her child; but Della—I left her sleeping beneath the shadow of the minarets."

Duncan stamped his foot. His cup of sorrow had been full. He had quaffed with what patience possible its bitter draughts, and still were they poured in afresh.

"I wrote you particulars of her death a year ago: I learned at Flat-Rock that you never have received the mournful tidings. I learned also"—but his voice trembled, and he could not go on.

"Of the sudden death of my wife. Good God! it may as well be spoken. Yes, she was to-day buried out of my sight."

"O, my friend, speak not with such wildness."

"But all is gone—all but dreary, wretched, useless life. O, what a world!"

"See here, my good brother," said the missionary, in a more cheerful tone, "I have come a long journey; I am tired to death, wet through, hungry, and cold."

Before he had finished, Duncan's hand had rang the bell violently. His right-hand man, Grandison, appeared. In a brief space of time, the fire was replenished, dry clothes produced, a small table of refreshments spread in the same cheery room, and the missionary, with commendable zeal, proceeded to refresh the inner man.

Duncan paced the floor in a desperate manner. The missionary paused amidst his slices of cold chicken and ham, and thus addressed him:

"My friend, I am greatly distressed for you, but that helps you nothing. I have been through the same fiery trial; and I not only believed, but wished I might not survive the ordeal. I would not eat nor sleep, but grieved incessantly. It was so sudden, so unforeseen. Was it not singular that Della and Ellice, loving each other so well, should have gone so near each other and in the same way? That is hardest of all; martyrs were they in a true sense. But I had a friend, who aroused, warned, and induced me to eat, sleep, and go on with the duties of life. After one first great effort it is easier. If one must suffer, he may assuage his pain by bearing it bravely. The over-tending of a wound may produce worst consequences. Exposure to the air, frequent ablutions, occasional frictions, create healing processes, reduce sensitiveness, and restore somewhat of the old life and vigor. I dare say you have not eaten a mouthful to-day; come eat, drink with me. I will not preach you a sermon, but let us philosophize like sensible men."

Thus solicited, Duncan drew up his chair opposite his friend. With evident disgust he swallowed the first mouthful, but this morsel seemed to awaken appetite, and he made a respectable meal.

Having thus broken his involuntary fast, he felt, in a sense, refreshed, and producing some fine cigars, the friends sat down before the fire, where, looking through the blue wreaths, they seemed to gain a soothing and an inspiration. The missionary gave to his host a brief history of his life with Della, of her sickness and death, and then incidentally gave a sketch here and there of his own youth. We will commence where he left off, giving but the substance in brief, instead of his own words, so often interspersed with irrelevant allusions and interrupted by remark and question.

Philip St. Leger was the son of a sea captain. His youth, of course, he spent mostly at school, its monotony varied more than once by a prolonged voyage with his father at sea. His mother was a woman of society, and left her children much to the care of servants. Consequently, she had much trouble with them in after years. Philip was the oldest child. He was naturally good-dispositioned and tractable; but, owing to a false system of training, became headstrong and altogether beyond maternal control.

At the age of nineteen, after a wild and fruitless career at college, and after repeated suspensions, he was really expelled near the beginning of the senior year. To his parents this was a severe mortification, and his father, being at that moment at home, sent him to some distant cousins, who lived among the white hills of New Hampshire.

Colonel Selby, in whose family Philip found himself domiciled, was a fine specimen of the country gentleman. Genial, hospitable, full of wit and anecdote, he was also a member of the Baptist Church, an ex-Senator of the United States, and ex-Governor of his own State. His eldest son was married, his youngest still in college, and his only daughter, about the age of twenty-two, was still an almost idolized child beneath her father's roof. The mother of these children had died a few years previously, and a widow from the city had supplied her place in the father's home and heart.

Philip St. Leger, black-haired, black-eyed, melancholy and romantic in look, cityfied and aristocratic in air and manner, attracted much attention among the simple people of the quiet town of Newberg. He could not help perceiving that, for the first time in his life, he had become a veritable lion. The very fact that he was Col. Selby's guest and relative gave to him importance; another fact, that he was the son of a wealthy sea captain from a distant city, was all-powerful.

It had indeed crept out somehow that he had been wild and extravagant, that he had been sent to rusticate among rocks and hills so sterile there would be little chance for his wild acts to take root; but then, to some old ladies and young ones too, this rumor lent but additional interest.

"Poor boy! what else could one expect? With such comeliness of person, endless wealth, unlimited advantages—the only wonder was he was not completely ruined." And he was compassionated and pitied for being obliged to remain in so old-fashioned and out-of-the-way country town as insignificant Newberg.

This pity was quite thrown away. Philip St. Leger was in his element; he had never been so happy in his life; Newberg was made up of hills, in the midst of grander mountains; it nestled in the western shadow of Keansarge; and King's Hill and Sunapee reared loftily around her their bold bleak fronts. A beautiful lake of the same name lay blue and clear at Sunapee's foot. "Pleasant Lake" lay in another direction, famous for its delicious trout and fragrant pond lilies.

Philip, the young scapegrace from city and from college, was in an ecstasy; he had never beheld skies so blue, lakes so fair, landscapes so lovely; with every breath he seemed to draw in life, vigor, and a new sense of beauty. Every morning he was up at sunrise, scouring the country upon the back of Nellie, a graceful, fleet young mare which Col. Selby had generously set aside for his use. Maids, matrons, and small boys stood in gaping amaze, stool in one hand and milk pail in the other, watching half-fearfully, half-admiringly, the fearless young equestrian, who shot by like a comet, his long, black hair streaming in the wind.

It was Philip's delight to create this stare and wonder, to which poor Nellie was obliged to contribute still more than her young master's pleasure. If he could leap over some low garden wall, dart over a famous strawberry bed, or amidst the melon patch, he thought he had done something splendid. The owner's dismay, not alone at the ruin, but at the untamed spirit that dared it, gave him peculiar delight.

Those old ladies who found their fattest goose dangling half-dead from the apple-bough in the early morning, or who looked in vain for patient cows within the yard, whose bars had mysteriously disappeared, began less to admire this youthful metropolitan.

Complaints poured in upon Col. Selby. At first he laughed and made light of them; then he consulted his wife. She was a staid, proper person, careful of the family's good name and popularity. It would never do. Philip ought to have some sense of what was due to his host; since he had not, he must be put in mind of it. She would undertake the task herself.

This she did, but without effect. Philip had promised sorrow and amendment with a long face, but inwardly he laughed, and after, became seven times worse than before.

Complaints multiplied. Not only were geese and cows interfered with, but dogs and horses were found tied to saplings or shut up in most unimaginable places. Burdocks and thistles appeared in meeting-house pews, where they surely had never before been known spontaneously to spring; teachers in the Sunday school were shocked to learn that they had distributed dime novels with books and tracts. The minister, one morning in the pulpit, solemnly opened his Bible, and unexpectedly beholding a most ludicrous picture, laughed outright, to the great scandal of every looker-on.

Now this was too much. Mrs. Selby had passed by stories of green-apple showers falling upon homeward-bound school children's heads; she had even smilingly held her peace when laughingly assured that a troop of dogs and cats had gone madly wailing and howling through the streets, a miniature world flaming with fire attached by means of wires to each caudal appendage—even that was too much decidedly. But this tampering with the meeting-house! Mrs. Selby consulted first her husband, as in duty bound; that is, she called him aside, told him the latest pranks of their protege, and emphatically added that there should be an end of them.

"But wife, I cannot turn the boy out of my house."

"You need not, my dear; that is my privilege, particularly since he is *my* relative, not yours. Forbearance now would cease to be a virtue; there is a limit to human endurance; there shall at once be an end to this boy's mad pranks. He is on the piazza, perhaps studying some new mischief; send him in to me, please."

"But are you not too hasty, wife?" urged the soft-hearted ex-Governor, who remembered his own follies and frolics of long ago.

"Too hasty, when we have all borne so much? Gov. Selby"—with a smile—"allow your wife to command you; send that naughty boy hither."

An hour later, Philip having sought her in house and garden, stood in presence of Mary Selby, at last discovered in her attic studio.

"Your mother has banished me; she has already spoken the fatal words; I must leave Newberg, this garden spot of God's glorious earth—most of all, I must leave you, cousin Mary, and I shall be lost, forever lost," exclaimed this strange youth, in tones melodramatic.

Mary laid aside her palette and brushes.

"Why then, cousin Phil, haven't you done better, after so many repeated warnings?"

"It is easy for *you* to ask that question, and you can answer it better than can I. Why do you not ask the wind why and whence it blows? Why do the waters overflow their banks, why ocean waves engulf life-freighted ships?"

"No, Philip, there is no analogy. Be reasonable; you are a being of will; you can do or not do. He is only a child who exercises no self-control, who is governed only by caprice, whim, or whatever passion of the moment. These follies, of which my mother makes account, and rightly, are beneath one of your age. There is in them nothing ennobling, charming; nothing that should gratify a mind that has the faintest conception of the good, the beautiful, and the true."

"I suppose so, cousin. But I have so long indulged in this fun-loving propensity"—

"That it has grown into an inveterate habit. Is this, then, a part of your better nature? Is there no depth beneath this evanescent surface—froth and foam? I believe there is. But in order that it may be discovered to the light and made fit for cultivation, this trivial surface-crust must be turned under, kept down, lest light and heat nourish its weeds into luxuriance."

"Why have you not talked to me thus before? *You* could do anything with me, cousin Mary."

"I will tell you the truth, Philip, because I think I owe it you. I went not with you to ride or walk, I have kept myself aloof from you, because my parents thought you too wild for my association."

"I am not a bear, and I might be better than I seem," said the proud boy, humbly.

"Yes, Philip, I believe you. And I have often thought I might do you good. Had you been my brother I should not have hesitated; but I had a suspicion that you might regard any persuasions or lectures from me as a piece of self-righteousness, for which you might have, as do I, supreme contempt."

"O, no, cousin. You are the best woman in the world. I would do anything for you."

"Leave off all of those mischievous pranks which are the cause of your present disgrace?"

"Yes, even that—and more. But it is too late now. I go to-morrow."

The result of this and still further conversation to the same effect produced a conviction upon the mind of Mary that the spoiled child was not beyond hope of redemption. She laid the case before her parents, and, with the aid of her father, obtained a reluctant consent from her mother that one more trial might be given the recreant Philip.

Even without this Mary would have gained her point, for on the next morning Philip, burning with fever, was unable to leave his bed.

A severe attack of typhoid ensued.

When Philip St. Leger, after a dangerous illness of many weeks, became convalescent, he was a changed person. Not alone through the influence of Mary, but Colonel Selby, and especially his wife, were brought to realize how prone they had been to reproach and condemn without having made the slightest efforts to reform. A neglected, untutored, un-Christianized young man had been placed in their care—was it too late to redeem the past? No effort was left untried, though exercised with the greatest delicacy to bring the young heathen's mind to a proper state of its former unhealthfulness, of its present pressing needs.

Mary read to him biographies of the good and great. She read ennobling works of poetry and counsel. She brought before his mind by example how superior was earnestness to trivialty, strict integrity to knavery and falsehood, goodness and piety to wickedness and infidelity. As she read and commented, her voice became to Philip as the voice of an angel. Her work was indeed accomplished when, after having listened to her rendering of St. Paul's grand epistles, there sprang up in his heart, first: "Almost thou persuadest me to be a Christian;" then this full, heart-swelling sympathy with the Apostle's words:

"For I am persuaded that neither death, nor life, nor angels, nor principalities, nor powers, nor things present, nor things to come, nor height, nor depth, nor any creature, shall be able to separate us from the love of God, which is in Christ Jesus our Lord."

CHAPTER V

THE MISSIONARY'S RETROSPECT

Though Philip St. Leger would have done, in almost all things, as Mary Selby directed, upon one certain point he was inflexible. This was upon the subject of immersion; he would not go down into the waters of Lake Sunapee, following the custom of the Newbergians.

During his boyhood his mother had been a member of the Presbyterian society; latterly, for some good reason or other, she had made a move into the Episcopal; whether through whim for popularity, or for conscience' sake was best known to herself. Her puritanical cousin, Mrs. Col. Selby, and a very worthy woman she was, regarded Mrs. St. Leger as a heretic, and looked upon the troubles with her children as a just punishment for having left the Church of her fathers. She had herself, however, meantime made very considerable concessions to her own religious convictions. For, while stoutly believing in sprinkling, in infant baptism, in open communion, and in each and every tenet of Presbyterianism, she had actually been received into the Calvinistic Baptist Church! What an unheard-of thing! It created no little talk among the good people of Newberg, and more for this reason: Mrs. Job Manning, a farmer's wife, who dutifully assisted her husband in earning a frugal living on the rocky sides of King's Hill, having been a Congregationalist, had been refused years previously, admittance to this same Church. She was poor, had a family of young children, had no way of traveling thirty miles to her own nearest meeting-house, and had humbly begged, with her husband, who was already a good Baptist, to be received into the Church. Failing this, since she could not consent to immersion, and shrank from the doctrine of close communion, she, or rather her husband, demanded that she might be allowed to partake occasionally of the Lord's Supper.

Rev. Mr. Savage, and the dignified Deacon Gould, and his equally dignified colleague, Deacon Drake, gazed very solemnly down upon the communion table, pursing up their mouths most decidedly, as if a sacrilege had already been committed by so astounding a proposition. Of course the duty fell upon Mr. Savage, the minister, to declare before all present that the demand of brother Manning, in behalf of his wife, was unreasonable, incomprehensible, and un-Christian.

Was Mrs. Manning a Christian? Then let her be baptized in a Christian manner, and thereby show herself worthy to eat the bread and drink the wine. Until such time there could be no admittance.

The two solemn-looking deacons on either side of the dogmatic speaker raised approvingly their eyes, and after balancing themselves a moment upon their toes, settled back upon their heels as grave and decorous as before.

Brother Job Manning arose hastily, and said:

"My wife, Nancy Manning, is as good a Christian woman as the town of Newberg holds. I eat with her at home, thank God, and if she ain't good enough to eat with me at the table of the Lord, then I ain't good enough neither, and you can have it all to yourselves."

And Job Manning, somewhat angry, it must be confessed, strode out from the assembled body of Christians, up to his pew in the side aisle, and plucking his wife by the sleeve, who arose and followed him, marched out of the Baptist church for good and all.

But in the case of Mrs. Colonel Selby it was altogether different. She was a woman of wealth and influence. She could do so very much for the Baptist church, it would never do to offend her. And the Colonel was so devoted to her, he might go off in a huff as poor Job Manning had done, and stand it out to the bitter end. It was a dilemma, no disputing about that. A bad precedent, more particularly after the precedent in the Manning case. But it *must* be got along with, and it *was*, and Mrs. Colonel Selby, a strict and ultra Presbyterian, always open and outspoken, became an honored member of this closely-guarded Baptist fold. What was to hinder? Who was to say, why do you so? No bishop with his interdict, no Pope with his "thunders from the Vatican." Here was one of the beauties of the Protestant system.

"System," says Webster, "is an assemblage of things adjusted into a regular whole, or a whole plan or scheme consisting of many parts connected in such a manner as to create a chain of mutual dependencies." It is not at all strange that Protestantism should protest against this definition, and should establish its own instead: An assemblage of things so adjusted and built up as that they may easily be rearranged or completely demolished as occasion may require, or a whole plan or scheme consisting of many parts so connected as to create a gossamer-thread of mutual independencies.

Mrs. Selby was too shrewd and sensible not to see the

inconsistency involved. But then she was quite used to inconsistencies. Moreover, she deemed herself quite in the right, and the Baptist Church had mounted upon the plane it behooved itself to stand; at all events, it must answer for its own right and wrong doing, as Mrs. Selby expected to answer for her own.

Mary Selby sought not to influence Philip in the matter of his baptism. She saw where his inclination tended and was silent. He accompanied his mother's cousin to her native city, and was there received into the First Presbyterian by Mrs. Selby's venerable and beloved friend, Rev. Mr. Storrs.

Colonel Selby used his influence in infringing upon the college rules of Dartmouth, and the young man, expelled from one college, was received into another. So bad use had he made of his former advantages that he was obliged to go back to the sophomore year; even here he had to study early and late to maintain his position.

After three years of assiduous diligence, he graduated with honor, when, for the first time since the day of his disgrace, he visited his paternal home.

His fashionable mother viewed her handsome, scholarly son, not only with amazement, but with pride and satisfaction. His three sisters, all grown into womanhood, the youngest being sixteen, were at first rather shy of him. They had not forgotten how he used to annoy and vex them. They early perceived the change, and became distressingly fond of him. It would be so nice to have an elder brother to go with them everywhere. And such a brother! so fine-looking, who had an air so distinguished, a face so poetical and classical! O, wouldn't all the other girls envy them this splendid brother? They would make a grand party, and exhibit him at once.

What was their dismay on finding that he absolutely refused to show himself to the guests! The wealthiest, most learned, most *elite* of the city were all in the drawing-rooms, beauty and fashion were in full glow and flow, music all atremble to stir into life, bright eyes were flashing expectation, and dainty lips had sweet words waiting to say, and he would not appear! In vain the mother coaxed, flattered, and got angry; in vain the sisters pleaded, begged, cried, and insisted. He was inexorable. But they had made the party on purpose for him!

Why had they not informed him sooner? He could have saved them all the trouble and disappointment. He could have told them he was no lion, and would not be paraded. He had not been in society for three years; he was never again going into society.

This, then, came of going off into the country! Buried alive. Come out so peerless and beautiful, and all to no purpose! He might just as well have been a grub!

By great efforts the mother and daughters choked down their wrath and mortification, bathed their swollen eyes, put on fresh lily white and carmine, and joined their guests. What should they have for an excuse? O, a sick headache—sudden and distressful—he was subject to them; poor Philip!

Later in the evening, Estelle St. Leger led Della Lisle up to her own room. They were passing through the hall. Opposite her door, Estelle stooped to lace her slipper, for which purpose she had left the drawing-room.

"So he has no headache," said Della, "and absents himself only from aversion to society?"

"That is all," replied Estelle, pettishly. "Isn't he stupid?"

"No, I just begin to think right well of him. I have no respect for some of those effeminate butterflies down stairs, who say only silly nothings, because, forsooth, they think we can appreciate nothing better, or because they have nothing better to offer."

"But I thought you were quite captivated with Edward Damon? You two, for the last half hour, have seemed to be unconscious that there was aught else in the world save that one corner that held you."

"Edward Damon is an exception. He is intelligent, unaffected, and agreeable. He is not all simper and softness. He can talk with one without being lost in his own self-conceit, fancying you deep in admiration of his own charming self. Yes, I really like Edward Damon."

The shoe was laced, and the girls passed on, but the voice of Della Lisle seemed still to linger upon the ears of Philip. His own door opened upon the hall very near to the waiting girls; he had heard every word. First, the voice of Della was pleasant and gentle; it powerfully attracted him; second, her words were not those of an ordinary city lady.

"A sensible girl, that—Della, Estelle called her; a pretty name. And Edward Damon is there, it seems, the best fellow I ever knew. Who knows? Maybe a shoe-string influences my fate. At all events, I am influenced in a way I may not resist."

And Philip St. Leger, with extraordinary inconsistency, soon appeared among his mother's guests. There was but one drawback to the joy and gratification of that mother and the three sisters—his necktie was not of the very latest style.

CHAPTER VI

MISSIONARY LIFE

In falling in love with Della Lisle at first sight, Philip pleased himself only and his sister Estelle; that is, if we leave Della out. His mother had the tall, graceful daughter of a millionaire selected for him; Leonora, the elder sister, had her pet friend Miss De Rosier, secretly engaged and under promise; Juliet, the younger, wished him never to fall in love, never to marry, but to remain forever her dear, only, adorable brother Philip, for whom she would give up all the world and live a maiden to the end of her life.

This engagement with Della, however, was not the worst that might be. They discovered this to their discomfiture when shortly after he announced to them one morning at the breakfast-table that on the following week he should leave for Princeton.

A theological course at Princeton! A true-blue Presbyterian, a long-faced, puritanical minister, who would deem it a sin to laugh, speak, or wink on a Sunday. And this was what their brother was coming to. This was why it had been impossible to get him to go with them to St. Mark's Church, though they had told him how beautifully *High* Church it was; how it had a high altar and candles, almost like the

Romanists, only that it was not at all Romish, but entirely and truly Catholic! Was ever such like woful perversity? When they had just got a brother to be proud of, who could take them to theatres, concerts, balls, operas, and everywhere, for him to go and degenerate into an old solemn Presbyterian minister! It would be bearable, if he must be a minister, if he would only be a High Churchman, and would be called a priest, and wear the surplice, and read the service in his charming voice, and be rector of such a fine, rich church as our own St. Mark's! They could put up with that, because he could still go with them to places of amusement, and would not be likely to scold them for dancing all night and sleeping all day. Besides, his praise would be in everybody's mouth, he would speedily get a D. D. to his name, the ladies would all admire him, and he would still be their own, own brother. They wished he had never seen Newberg, nor Colonel Selby's family, nor Dartmouth College. They forgot or were ungrateful for his transformation from a state of good-for-nothingism to comparative Christian virtue.

Philip perceived and was pained at the folly and frivolousness of his mother's household, but any attempt at change more favorable appeared to him so herculean, that he made scarcely an effort in its behalf. He was conscious that therein lay neglect of duty; they might owe to him what he owed to Mary Selby. Often when he thought of her he bowed his head reverently, and said: I have two saviours—an earthly and a heavenly—Mary Selby and my Lord and Saviour Jesus Christ.

To the near relatives of Philip his going to Princeton was so much like burying him, that when, after three years, he returned finally to his home and announced that in one month he was both to marry and sail as missionary to Turkey they were scarcely surprised. They made no outcries and no ado; they had given him up long ago; he would be no company for them in their rounds of gaiety and fashion; he might as well be teaching heathens or Musselmen in the kingdoms of the Brother to the Sun as a dry, dull parson in America, ever in danger of offending their aristocratic tone and ideas by his sober, old-fashioned notions.

After his marriage, before embarking for Turkey, Philip, with his bride, paid a visit to Newberg. His second sermon he preached in the Baptist church. To those simple-minded country people, he stood before them a living illustration of what the grace of God might effect. Six years previously he had startled and amazed them, as though he had ridden through the air on a broomstick; now he came back to them in peace and gentleness. Before he had laid sacrilegious hands upon the Holy Bible in the sacred pulpit; now he opened the same reverently and read from thence the words of eternal life. The change was indeed marvellous, and Newberg proudly set him down as a second Paul the Apostle.

Della was dreadfully seasick on the ocean voyage, and, as she often declared, it seemed she never became completely well again. Owing to this delicate state of her health, the St. Legers did not accompany their companions to the field assigned them, a small town in the interior, but remained in Constantinople, at the house of Dr. Adams, resident Protestant minister of that city.

It was not until after the birth and death of her first child, when her health became somewhat reinstated, that Della was able to accompany her husband to their contemplated mission. Here they rejoined their companions of a year ago; Mr. and Mrs. Fisher, and Mr. and Mrs. Dodd. It had been a former mission until recently abandoned; the houses, small and inconvenient at best, had either been appropriated or fallen to decay.

A few rooms had been made habitable, and here the missionaries had taken up their abode. Cheerless it seemed and disheartening to Philip and Della, as they saw no progress at all made in the objects of their long journey, but every effort consumed in struggles for daily bread.

"What have you been doing?" asked the St. Legers, so wonderingly as to convey almost a reproach.

"The same as yourselves," retorted the Fishers and the Dodds, "nursing our healths to make us well."

"We will all begin together then," said Philip pacifyingly.

"As soon as you please; you shall lead and we will follow," answered the associates.

Notwithstanding this ebullition of energy at the outset, month after month, nay, year after year elapsed without the least material progress. What was termed a school would be sometimes kept up for weeks together, at which some few children could be coaxed to come; but after the supply of pictures, ornaments, etc., with which they had been attracted gave out, the attendance languished and the idle urchins sought amusement elsewhere.

Bibles were flung out with a lavish hand to men, women, and children who had never before possessed such a treasure as a book; and this book might for them just as well have been a bundle of old almanacs, for all printed language was Greek to them. And they, these missionaries, did not believe that the mere possession of the holy word of God could impart or draw down God's grace upon the possessor; for that would be akin to the miraculous, and they eschewed faith in miracles.

An attempt was made at expounding and hearing the word of God on Sundays. There was good enough will in these expositions, but the ears and the hearts for receiving were far away. People, it is true, would come some days in crowds, but it was not for instructions; they went as young America goes to see a band of turbaned Turks, or Barnum's latest humbug.

Where was the use of spending so many persons' energies upon such a stolid, indifferent, intractable people? They were wedded to their idols, why not leave them alone? Why should they cast pearls before swine?

These were questions the missionaries asked themselves; and answered too, if not to their satisfaction, to the best of their ability. Their time became more and more consumed in the care of their increasing families.

These missionaries in their home-reports might well speak of hardships. The women were often sick, help could but rarely be obtained, and then of the poorest quality; thus these gentlemanly graduates of Yale, Dartmouth, and Princeton had often not only to cook meals for the family, but to wash, iron, attend the sick wife and helpless infants, and suffer all the anxieties and annoyances that human flesh is heir to. What wonder that they came gradually to lose sight of the grand aspirations that had animated their early manhood? To forget, as it were, the objects and aims of their holy mission, and to sink into the mere *paterfamilias*, like other good masters of families? There seemed no alternative; the routine of domestic duties must be accomplished; the sick must be attended to; hungry mouths must be fed, fast-coming forms must be clothed. Where was the time to go forth seeking the heathen or compelling him to come in? The wife and children could neither be taken nor left alone. In fact, the missionaries found to their great surprise, as all experienced men have found, that the care of a family is a never-ceasing, all-engrossing responsibility. The outside work could be very small indeed; all had to centre in that one spot, home. They cultivated small gardens, and in this way eked out their subsistence on the small salaries received from the Board of Missions.

Thus lived they from year to year, hopeless of the present, but overflowing with hopes for the future. Though they could labor not *now* in Christ's vineyard, they might do so by and by; though they might live to behold no fruit of their labors, they might, unknown even to themselves, have sown the good seed, and their children's children, and the children of heathendom might arise up and call them blessed.

Della Lisle's life—or rather Della St. Leger's—in the land of her adoption, lasted but five years; she had buried two little children, who, so brief was their existence, could scarcely be said to have lived at all. As her third trial was approaching and her health in wretched state it was deemed best that she should be taken by easy stages to Constantinople, where English medical advice could be procured. The journey proved invigorating, and Della landed at Dr. Adams' in almost as good health as when she had left, more than four years previously.

There was always good company at the house of Dr. Adams. English and American travelers, whether religious or not, were wont to claim his hospitality.

Upon the arrival of the St. Legers, a very interesting gentleman was spending a few days; he bore the common name of Chase, but he was no common man. Though still in the prime of life, he had traveled the world over, made himself conversant with all languages, manners, and customs, studied into all fanaticisms and all religions, and if he had ended in having faith in none, as such people often do, he admirably kept his own counsel.

After coffee, the Doctor with his guests withdrew to the open court; distributing a Turkish pipe to each, he sat himself down upon his cushion, prepared to listen to this traveled friend with his usual animation.

Dr. Adams' house being head-quarters for missionaries coming and going, and Philip St. Leger being at this time the third who had arrived within a day or two, the others being still present, the conversation naturally turned upon missionary life.

Now, Mr. Chase was a Yankee; and though a cultivated one, he had not parted with an innate inquisitiveness, and had an off-hand way of asking such questions as first presented. He catechised these three missionaries as faithfully, even in presence of Dr. Adams, as if he had been President of the American Board. He desired to know the number of years spent in the work, the size and extent of their missions, the number of actual converts, and also all about their own families and modes of living.

Having apparently satisfied himself, Mr. Chase said, wheeling around to the Doctor:

"The same story. In my various travels I have come frequently across these missionary stations; you will pardon me if I tell you what you cannot fail to know, that they are complete failures. In my opinion, the money might be better expended in planting gunpowder."

The three youthful missionaries opened wide their eyes, but the Doctor smoked away complacently.

CHAPTER VII

THE DISTINGUISHED TRAVELER'S VIEWS

Mr. Chase dropped his pipe, as if in a great hurry, and continued:

"Now, here are three missionaries, and they will excuse me, as I am about to present to them a great truth—each of whom has left at his respective station from two to four colleagues. There are then from ten to fifteen men, with as many women and more children; the difficulty is with these women and children; they are very dear, precious objects, I have no doubt, in their own homes and in Christian lands, but they are only clogs and drawbacks in such an enterprise as these young men are engaged. A man alone can dive into forests, scale mountains, swim rivers, fight lions, eat raw birds, make his bed in caves, or on solid rock, lie down with the Indian, rise up with the Hindostan, do any and every conceivable wild outlandish thing that the world's nations do; but with a woman—pshaw, that alters the case."

"But there are instances of brave women," remarked the Doctor, "Look at Lady Hester Stanhope, and Lady—"

"But they were unmarried women. There are the Amazons of old too, and Amazons are not wanting at the present time—

but such do not come within my category. From the very nature of the case, a man with a wife is fettered; he cannot be absent from home twenty-four consecutive hours. She is afraid of the dark, afraid of dogs and lions, of robbers and murderers, afraid the children will get sick, or that 'something or other will be sure to happen, as always does if he is away.' He too is as uneasy as herself, meditates all sorts of mishaps, imagines the house on fire, Johnny in the well, Fanny with a bean in her throat or a corn in her ear, and is on thorns and briers until his own house circles him around again. This is all right and natural for the ordinary domestic man; but, as I understand it, the missionary undertakes God's work; he renounces the world, its joys, comforts, friendships; he is no longer his own; but his will, love, obedience, and work is all for God, his Master, and for the heathen who know Him not. The truth is, the man who considers himself called to missionary labors should leave his wife behind him; that is, he should have no wife."

The Doctor, who was now a man of sixty, had been thrice married, and was now entertaining thoughts of a fourth wife, took his pipe from his lips and said emphatically:

"You are an extremist, Mr. Chase, you speak thus perhaps because it has been your lot to lead a single life; but, let me tell you, I think our missionaries sacrifice enough, without being obliged to come wifeless among negroes, Hindoos, South-sea islanders, and Cannibals. A dreary life at best— unendurable without companionship. You wouldn't get a man to sail under the conditions you propose."

"Did the Apostles have wives and children pulling after them?" continued Mr. Chase. "Imprisoned, stoned, beaten, and scoffed, was their life less dreary than should be the missionary's of to-day? What says St. Paul—'thrice was I stoned, thrice was I beaten with rods, thrice I suffered shipwreck, a night and a day have I been in the deep.' Do you suppose it ever occurred to that mighty, God-like spirit, even in the lowest depth of his worldly misery, that it would be a comfort to have a wife come to weep with him, to hand him fresh gown and sandals? Never so far fell that grand soul from its exalted repose upon the bosom of the infinite! From that source whence he drew courage sublimer, faith diviner, and strength irresistible, which no woman's heart or hand could aid in evoking! Ah, that was a glorious St. Paul."

"You are eloquent, sir, as all of us might well be over such a subject," said the Doctor; "but you must remember that only one St. Paul has ever lived."

"Though he has been a model for many. I don't know—only *one* St. Paul? I think if we look back into history—say, take the Fathers of the Desert—there was St. Jerome, a grand old man, St. Augustine, with less of fire, but of lofty faith, St. Ephrem, there, in him you have a St. Paul in eloquence; you will remember that his words were wont to flow so rapidly that his frequent exclamation was—'O Lord, stay the tide of Thy grace.' Why, the number is countless whose labors, toils, and self-denials were gigantic. St. Benedict, St. Wilfred, St. Bernard stand out—"

The Doctor having thrown down his pipe and commenced walking the floor, here interrupted his enthusiastic guest:

"O, if you go to taking up the Roman Catholic calendar of Saints, you will find plenty of fish in illimitable waters; but that is out of our line of coasting, you must know; and we are not in the habit of associating St. Paul with any of these latter-day Saints."

"Please allow me, Dr. Adams, you know I am a privileged person. My last-named Saint, Bernard, lived at least four hundred years before Luther and John Knox, and Wilfred and Benedict much nearer to Christ than to us, the latter having been separated in time but four centuries from his Lord; but let us not contend upon this point; I cheerfully admit my own superior admiration for the converted persecutor of the Christians."

"If his like has not been seen through eighteen hundred years, we may not look for it in the nineteenth century," remarked the Doctor.

"I still insist, however," said the indomitable Mr Chase, "that he has had many imitators; and that brings us back to the subject whence we have strayed, and upon which I have not said all that I had intended. I was going to remark, after asserting that missionaries should leave their wives at home, that the success of Catholic missionaries illustrates the truth of this."

"I beg you to remember," interposed the Doctor, testily, "that we do not wish to be compared in any way, shape, or manner with the Catholic missionaries. You might just as well compare us to the heathen who worship idols."

Mr. Chase continued, a little more mildly than before:

"The question is not, my dear Doctor, a comparison between your religion and theirs. I understand very little indeed about their religion. But their object and yours is the same; by every means in your power to induce souls ignorant of the Saviour to believe and accept the truths you hold out; this is your mission, and this is theirs. You come with your families, you make a home—you stay there—waiting for the heathen to come to you; your wife is nervous, she likes not the uncouth looks and ways of your barbarians; she is neat and she does not like her white floor to be soiled by the dirty feet of your savages. Nervous, neat, and timid herself, she meets their gaze anything but smilingly—even savages are human, and know well enough how to take a hint. Her involuntary dislike is returned with interest, and her husband's influence and usefulness is at an end, even before being established."

"You judge us harshly," complained Dr. Adams, glancing at the dissatisfied countenances of his younger friends, "some missionaries have most excellent wives."

"Do not understand me as saying one word against any missionary's wife; far be it from me. As a class, I have no doubt they are most estimable. But women are women all the world over, and experience convinces me that in the place they occupy as wives of missionaries they are only greatly in the way. Now the Roman Catholics—and I am no friend to their religion, as you very well know—as missionaries, are those only who have met with success. *They* attribute it to the grace of God following their efforts, in accordance with the divine promise, 'Go teach all nations, and lo, I am with you to the end of the world.' I have visited their missions in every part of the world; in North and South America, in Africa, Europe, Asia, and many islands of the sea—and in fact this really did confound me, though I have been almost everywhere under the sun, these missionaries were already there, working away as for dear life—well, as I was saying, I have been in many a place where, to get the least comfort at all, I was compelled to put up with them; and, I always went away soothed, refreshed, and consoled. I assure you it is wonderful; they go among the natives, and to a certain extent become one of them; they win their confidence, treat them kindly, share with them food and drink, sleep in their houses and tents, and by and by insensibly have become their masters. Then how easy to teach them anything! Now they couldn't do this with troops of women and children along; so

I came to the conclusion that their remarkable success in the conversion of heathen nations was to be attributed to the absence of these hindering appendages."

"But you must have found nuns as missionaries in some places."

"You know they are invisible to us profane people. They do have charge of schools in some missions—but then, cannot you perceive that a dozen of nuns, independent and self-supporting, is a very different institution from a dozen of married women and half a dozen dozen small responsibilities?"

The Doctor laughed good-humoredly.

"You stick to your point like the bark to a tree," he said. "What do you say, young gentlemen," addressing his silent, but ill-pleased guests, "are you convinced that you have made a blunder, and are you ready to set about retrieving it?"

St. Leger answered, with a voice that slightly trembled with indignation:

"I am convinced, Dr. Adams, that the learned gentleman who is so conversant with the subject of missions, should seek and find his true and proper position in the bosom of those successful idolaters he so greatly admires."

"Why, you take it to heart," said the Doctor. "Had you known Mr. Chase as long and well as I have, you would make a different estimate of his remarks;" and he turned the subject, for, in truth, he was not at all pleased with these plainly spoken views, deeming them entirely uncalled for and inapropos. He hastened to call out the distinguished traveler upon a less distasteful theme.

CHAPTER VIII

THE VISITATION—BY SPIRIT AND BY DEATH

When Philip retired to his room that night he was surprised to find his wife still awake. "What a wonderful man that is who has been entertaining you this evening," she said.

"Wonderful fool!" ejaculated the pious missionary, whose disturbed temper had not yet become altogether serene.

Della was quite thrown back by so unwonted an exclamation, and remained silent. At length Philip said:

"What do you know about him? where have you seen him? haven't you spent the whole evening in this room?"

"Yes, but the windows open upon the court; I have heard every word."

"And heard no good of yourself, either," remarked Philip, snappishly.

Her husband was in so unusual a mood that Della hesitated about entering upon the conversation she had intended. She was impulsive, however, and did not like to wait.

"Philip, I want to say something," said she, gently.

"Well, say away," was his ungracious permission.

"I thought you had something to say," he said again, more gently, as Della remained silent.

"It was only this: I had been thinking the same thing," she said, almost in a whisper.

Now Philip knew very well what his wife meant. *He*, too, had thought the same thing. But he pretended to be in the dark, and abruptly demanded:

"The same *what* thing? Why must you speak so enigmatically?"

"O, Philip, you could have done so much more and better without me. I have done nothing, and have hindered you."

"And what are you going to do about it?" said Philip, coldly.

"Why, Philip, what *is* the matter with you? How strangely you answer me!" cried Della, excitedly.

"Never mind me now, Della I am not myself to-night; go to sleep."

Truly, thought Della, he is not himself; so she prudently resolved to defer her "something to say" to a more favorable season.

For the next eight or nine hours Philip's mind was in a whirlpool. While a student at Princeton, the lectures of Cardinal Wiseman had chanced to fall in his way. He read them with avidity, particularly those "On the Practical

Success of the Protestant Rule of Faith in Converting Heathen Nations," and "On the Practical Success of the Catholic Rule of Faith in Converting Heathen Nations." They left upon his mind unpleasant impressions, and created doubts and misgivings which his tutors could with difficulty dispel. But he shut his eyes, blinded his mind, and allowed the hour of his visitation to pass by. Now, the words of this Mr. Chase, a stray traveler, roaming through the world without aim or object, so far as known, had aroused this slumbering phantom of the past, and provoked, if not challenged, him anew. He recalled the story of Catholic missions that had read to him like a continuation of Apostolic labors; statistics, gathered altogether from Protestant sources, showed them to be overwhelmingly successful; the gift of miracles and the gifts of the Holy Ghost had descended upon them, and crowns of martyrdom numerous and shining. He had even thought with a thrill that had he never met Della it would be glorious to join this lion-hearted band, whose symbol was the ever-upborne Cross! But there had avalanched down upon this temporary glow such a storm of ridicule against Transubstantiation, worship of the Blessed Virgin and of dead men's bones and cast-off garments, and the putrified corruptions of the Man of Sin generally, that the one generous, struggling spark was extinguished. Of the great Protestant Foreign Missionary Society, for which so much money had been expended, so many millions of Bibles distributed, so many glowing reports printed, Philip St. Leger was now a part, knew all its ins and outs—alas! its outs.

This was the reason Mr. Chase's remarks had so fretted him: because of the truth which he was unwilling to receive. To himself this young missionary had admitted long before that a married man was too much cumbered for his undertaking. At the same time he mentally insisted that in that foreign land life without his wife would be to him intolerable. It was truly distressing and discouraging that five years had passed by with but the most trifling results. He thought, and not for the first time, that were he settled in the faraway, quiet village of Newberg, his life might not pass away so unprofitably. But he had put his hand to the plough; should he now turn back?

The dissatisfied missionary passed a sleepless night; he murmured and repined; he was not willing to ascribe praise to his Roman Catholic brethren, nor to admit their right to claim the promise of our Lord to be with them unto the end. The result was that he resisted the spirit, and allowed this second visitation to pass by, leaving him more self-determined than before. Therefore, with the dawn of day, he resolutely dismissed the subject, with emphasis asserting: "I am a Protestant; I will live and work with my Protestant brethren. We must admit nothing on the part of our adversaries; we must make our claims as bold as theirs."

When, therefore, a few days after, Della renewed the subject, he was prepared to quiet her scruples.

"And is their success, then, so really wonderful as this gentleman declares?" she inquired.

"Not at all. Doubtless in many places they do gain a temporary success, but this is easily accounted for. The Catholic religion lies in outward observances. They have so much show and ceremony that the ignorant native is necessarily attracted. The dress, altar, lights, bell, all have their part in alluring the curious. They think there must be some great mystery connected with so much paraphernalia. They are naturally willing to be let into the secret. But there is nothing in it at all to convert the heart or convince the understanding. When these useless accessories are removed, the converted heathen, as he is called, relapses into barbarism."

"It has seemed to me, though, Philip, that if we had only something in our service to attract the attention, we would have a great advantage; that is the first and principal thing to get people together. By having something to win their curiosity, a great point is gained. Giving them a Bible is like giving them a stone for bread—they can make nothing out of it," said Della, decidedly.

"But when they have the teachings of the Bible once thoroughly impressed upon their minds, does it not stand to reason they would be better and more persevering Christians?" asked Philip.

"Very likely. But the difficulty is to make this impression. We tell the heathen, man, woman, or child, that Christ died on the Cross to redeem us. Would he not lend us more earnest attention if we illustrated our instruction by exhibiting to him an image of the Cross and the Crucified— in short, if we taught him, as did the ancients, the whole story of Redemption, and the establishment of the Church, by series of pictures and images?"

"What is the use of going back thousands of years ago when we are living in the nineteenth century? Why not make use of the art of printing since we have it?"

"Certainly, wherein it is of advantage. But the majority of those whom the missionary seeks to instruct are beyond the reach of that admirable art. Letters have for them no meaning; books are for them only to look at; and with a picture the eye is instructed and more pleased."

"Let us send to Rome for a cart-load of Madonnas, crucifixes, beads, and all the et ceteras for satisfying and perpetuating superstition and ignorance," said Philip, sarcastically.

Della was sensitive to ridicule and remained silent. Her husband continued:

"Or, since you deem yourself a supernumerary in your present vocation, suppose you allow me to pack you off in the return-cart to the Eternal City, that is said to sit over the mouth of Il Inferno. You may kiss the toe of his Holiness, and humbly ask penance for the rest of your mortal life for having presumed to be a Protestant missionary's wife, and carried the Bible to the dying heathen."

"The subject is too serious for any such nonsense," remarked the wife, gravely. "The question is *how* to convert the heathen. It seems to me the true missionary of the Cross should not be above receiving prudent suggestions from whatever source; more particularly ourselves, who are inexperienced in the work."

"You are right, Della, as you always are," replied the husband, more sincerely. "I have been revolving the subject over, and have come to a firm resolution to turn over a new leaf on our return to the mission. If Mrs. Fisher were not so peevish and Mrs. Dodd so distressingly particular, we could get along better in the kitchen; the native girls would do better, and improve. If you were to oversee that department, I think there would be a change greatly for the better. The truth is, I believe those women are afraid of being poisoned. They ought to give their time in the school. If they tried to make it interesting there would be a better attendance. It is all nonsense to spend one's whole time in getting up dainty dishes, and *recherche* toilets for one's babies. At all events we must arouse ourselves from this slough of indifference and give our best energies to the work. We have not made half a trial yet. How can we expect success to follow aught but energetic effort?"

Distance lent enchantment. Now that the missionaries were hundreds of miles away, the labors of the mission seemed easy of accomplishment, and the daily, hourly difficulties and hindrances dwindled into insignificance.

Scarcely a month later and Philip St. Leger bent in thankfulness over a little daughter, which the doctor said might live.

"We will call her Della," said Philip to his wife.

"Not Della, but Althea. I give her to God, Philip. May she do for Him what I have not been able."

Philip had turned to his wife that he might the better catch her feeble whispers. O, the dread that rushed through his heart! A ghastly pallor was spread over the face, a convulsive spasm distorted for a moment the sweet mouth.

"I am going—O, Philip," she said, wildly, and ere he had time to call on God for mercy she was gone.

"Good God, doctor, is she really dead?" cried Philip, as soon as he could speak to the physician upon the opposite side, whose fingers now let fall the pulseless wrist.

"All is over," answered the physician, sadly.

"Why did you not call me sooner if you saw the danger? How dared you not inform me at once?" demanded Philip.

"Pray be quiet, my dear sir. It was very sudden—entirely unanticipated—although I had been suspecting disease of the heart. Her lungs were a good deal affected, but her heart I think the immediate cause of her death. Otherwise, she was doing nicely, bravely, better than could be expected. You have met with a great loss, sir—a wonderful loss—your wife was a noble woman. God help you!"

Della St. Leger was buried by the side of the first and third Mrs. Adams, the second having been buried on an island in the sea. The latter had been a Southern lady, and had brought with her a colored woman, at that time her slave. This person, Minerva by name, remained still an invaluable member of Dr. Adams' household. To her care the little motherless Althea was entrusted; and Philip St. Leger, with what heart may be imagined, went back alone to his dreary mission.

CHAPTER IX

THE NEW CHOICE

We have given a more thorough retrospect of the missionary's antecedents than did he to his friend on that memorable night at Kennons. But the gleam of his flashing eye, and the glow of the sparkling flame into which he gazed was like flint to flint; and to us was it given mysteriously to read the fiery flashes thus revealed.

From the death of Della, he went on to inform his brother-in-law that he had brought back his child in care of the faithful Minerva, whom he had left with his younger sister for the present. He did *not* tell him that the real object of his present visit to America was to take to himself a wife for the second time. This, however, he might, have told, had he not found his friend in such affliction, as that any news of this kind must have grated upon him harshly.

Indeed, several months previously he had written to the principal of the Seminary for her to select a suitable young lady for his future wife. This was not the first time her offices had been solicited in this line; but she was an elderly lady, sensible and practical, and naturally thought that a missionary's second wife should be distinguished for something more than youth and beauty.

Accordingly, when, upon Philip's arrival in his native city, he had visited his friends, and disposed of his daughter, he called upon Madame X—, she presented to him her choice for Mrs. St. Leger, in the person of Miss Arethusa Toothaker, the eldest, tallest, most sedate young lady of her establishment.

Miss Toothaker was of an uncertain age, though she called herself twenty-seven—was tall, as we have said, and slender, had a long, narrow head, which she carried on a neck too long, had very red cheeks, small snapping black eyes, very thin hair, of which she wore in front two very meagre curls done in cork-screw style, held her broad shoulders high, as if vainly striving to get them far as possible from her long, ant-like waist—well, this is enough, for at the very first glance Philip St. Leger turned away his eyes and closed his heart.

Upon taking his leave Philip informed Madame that Miss Toothaker would not do.

Madame was surprised; "She would make a worthy companion," insisted the principal, "and the dream of her life has been to become the wife of a missionary."

The missionary smiled—he would not disturb her dreams for the world—but "would Madame X—allow him to be present at the morning exercises of the school some day?"

"Certainly, any morning you please—to-morrow, if agreeable, you can open school with prayer and address some useful remarks to the young ladies."

On the following morning was great commotion in the ranks of the young ladies. The handsome, distinguished foreign missionary was to open school. At the "let us pray," a hundred young heads rested upon the upraised right hand;

but it is to be feared that authorized devotional attitude was sadly infringed upon, for, when he pronounced "Amen" sooner than was anticipated, he encountered so many bright admiring eyes that a less self-possessed person than Philip might have been abashed. As our hero had studied his speech, however, he was able to commence and go through without the slightest embarrassment. His keen eye swept the array of youth and beauty before him, and so quick was he in arriving at conclusions, his choice was made before his remarks were ended.

A person of less penetration might have chosen many another than Emily Dean. There were several among her compeers of more beauty and brilliance. But Philip St. Leger was a good judge of character; he had but to look upon a face to read the heart. He had loved Della Lisle from hearing her voice, and from one glance at her countenance. Emily Dean wore her hair, like hers also in color and abundance, as had Della. In this only was resemblance, unless in a certain pensiveness of expression and pose of attitude.

Madame X—was again surprised, when, in the afternoon of the same day, the missionary asked for an interview with "the young lady who had occupied the fifth seat on the right hand side of the third row, who wore her hair somewhat like a crown, and was dressed in pale blue."

"Ah! Emily Dean—a very fine girl—but is she not too young—hardly nineteen?"

"I myself am not a Methuselah," remarked the missionary, somewhat piqued that although but thirty-one, he should be esteemed too unsuitably old for even the youngest of Madame X—'s pupils.

"Of course—O certainly—of course—I beg your pardon,"

said the lady hastily, "but a missionary's wife, you know—there is much to be considered."

Philip, evidently bent upon doing his own considering, pursued his inquiries, and gained the interview. He proposed to the young lady in presence of the principal, and in so very business-like a way as convinced both the elder and the younger that there was more practicability beneath that poetical exterior, than the latter would have suggested or warranted them in believing.

Philip was not long in discovering Emily Dean to be the eldest child of an independent farmer in Western New York. She had four sisters and three brothers younger than herself. "With such a family, the father can more easily part with this daughter," thought Philip; and he started off on the next train to visit the family of the Deans.

Emily he found to be a favorite in the household. His proposition to take her with him "away to the barbarous Turk" was received with consternation and tears. The more, that it was felt, from the first, that if she wished it they should have to give her up.

The enthusiastic suitor proposed the father should at once go for his daughter and conduct her home. To all objections and demurrers as to haste and postponement Philip had a ready and eloquent answer. There was no gain-saying this ardent pleader.

The farmer left his host of potato-gatherers and apple-pickers and went off on the express. In twenty-four hours he returned with his daughter. Philip would have given no time for preparations—but in this he was forced to yield.

The parents insisted their eldest daughter should have a

wedding *trousseau*—it was not meet she should set out on so long a voyage, across the ocean of water, and the ocean of married life, in the condition of Miss Flora McFlimsey. So Philip St. Leger took this interval of time for his flying trip to his brother-in-law in Virginia.

But he found, as we have seen, the gloom of death spread over Kennons. Had he needed aught to convince him anew of the evanescent nature of all beneath the sun, he found it here. It was indeed painful to contrast the joy and happiness of this Southern home of little more than six years ago, and the present desolation. In that joy he had shared—in this gloom was his own heart wrung. In the moment of mournful silence that followed his long; discourse and Duncan's, life seemed to him not worth the living, and rising from his chair he said, with marked emphasis:

"Duncan, my friend, we are but travelers of a day. Our life, like that fire, goes out in ashes. The night comes, and we sleep. *Do* we rise again? Does this corruption put on incorruption—this mortal put on immortality? O, could I hear a voice from Heaven say unto me '*Yes*,' I should be comforted!"

"Why, Philip! Have you, too, doubts? God Almighty help us, when the faith of His ministers falters!"

"Bear with me now, Duncan; the darkness in my soul is deep and terrible to-night; death and the grave seem the only sure certainties we have in this world. Morning may bring me right again, if another morning remain for me. Let us sleep— and good night!"

The friends separated—and Duncan pondered on the missionary's last words. They seemed prophetic; and he almost expected, when he sent Grandison to his room on the following morning, to see that servant return with direful news. Not so. Philip appeared about ten o'clock, declaring he had slept well, and felt much refreshed. He remained for several days at Kennons, during which time the grave of Ellice was opened, and a tiny coffin let down upon her own; mother and child were re-united; and as Philip offered a prayer over the fresh-thrown earth, a ray of stronger faith enkindled his heart. Philip talked of his own little girl to Duncan Lisle:

"I had intended leaving her with my sister Estelle, who was my favorite. She was much attached to Della," said Philip; "But I found Estelle's husband does not like children; besides, she has three of her own, the eldest but a baby, and twins younger. Leonora is well married, but devoted to society, has no children of her own, and no idea of being troubled with other people's. I could not leave her with my mother, even though she had not been an invalid. My only resource was to entrust her with Juliet, who was but recently married, and who, with her husband, received the child delightedly. I do not feel at all satisfied with the arrangement, but it was the best I could do. Juliet is good-hearted, over-affectionate, and will be kind to the child; but she is rather simple-minded, frivolous, and variable. Her husband is a kind, sensible man, but he was raised a Roman Catholic. Juliet tells me that he is not much of anything now; but I doubt it, for he insisted on being married by the priest, before the ceremony at St. Mark's; and then again, the idea of one who has been raised a Catholic ever being anything else *but* a Catholic. It is preposterous. I have charged Juliet to see that no influence is ever brought to bear upon the mind of my child as she advances in years—but I have still grave fears. Possibly the time may come when you can remove her to Kennons, say, for a year or so, at a time; it would be a source of pleasure to me to have Althea beneath the roof under which her excellent mother was reared."

Duncan but too gladly promised to keep an oversight of the child; he would occasionally visit her during her infancy, and his home should ever be open to her; had Ellice lived she should have known no other.

The friends, newly attached, took sad leave of each other. Duncan leaned upon the gate, and watched the other as he rode slowly through the lane. Had the feet of the horse been mounting stairs that led upward to the skies, Duncan would not have felt more sure that Philip was passing forever from his view.

"Traveling, he one way, I another, yet both to the same goal—eternity," mused Duncan.

As he spoke, a carriage came in view, hiding the retreating traveler. He discerned at a glance that the carriage, drawn by fiery, coal-black steeds, was that of Mrs. Rush, He remained by the gate until the driver drew rein, and the bright, glowing face of the lady put itself out of the window.

"So, Mr. Lisle, your friend has already gone. I had no idea he was going so soon. I am so sorry. I was going to have had you over to dinner to-day. As it is, you can come, Mr. Lisle,—you and Hubert."

Duncan Lisle pleaded indisposition, and politely declined.

"But what are you going to do? House yourself up and mope yourself to death?" persevered the handsome widow. "I know how it is, and that you must feel a disinclination to society; but one must make an effort, you know. Come, I will take you right over in my carriage; there is plenty of room. Come, Hubert, come, jump in;" and the little boy, very willing, sprang up to the side of the carriage. His father went to assist him.

"Hubert may go, but, really, I cannot, Mrs. Rush. You must excuse me. Another time, perhaps."

"But I don't excuse you, Mr. Lisle. I am so disappointed You know what a splendid cook my Dinah is, and I ordered her to do her best. But then I suppose if you won't, you won't, and there's an end of it; is that so?"

"That is so, Madam," and touching his hat gracefully, he bade her an inaudible "good-morning," and turned away.

Mrs. Rush ordered Washington, her coachman, to drive home. She was disappointed and chagrined, but not discouraged. She was vain as a peacock or Queen Elizabeth. Like another *Dorcasina*, she fancied every man to be her *inamorata*. She had never abandoned the idea that Duncan Lisle had been once in love with her. She had been encouraged in this delusion by the duplicity of her servants, who, to propitiate her favor, had been in the habit of repeating false expressions of his admiration and regard.

"If all reports are true, he thinks more of you this day than he does of Miss Ellice," said one.

"Everybody knows that Duncan Lisle worships the ground you tread on, and always did. Miss Ellice happened to come along and just inveigled him, that is all; he is sorry enough, you may 'pend," falsified another.

"He always *was* talking about how mighty han'some you was, and what beautiful eyes you had," declared a third, and so it went, and credulous Mrs. Rush laid the flattering unction to her soul that she was the one woman in the world for Duncan Lisle.

"It is only for looks' sake; he wanted to come bad enough,

you may bet on that," said Dinah to her mistress, when informed that she had got up her great dinner for nobody but little Master Hubert.

As to Hubert, after he was through with his good dinner, he had anything but a pleasant visit. Thornton Rush—his name was Jude Thornton Rush—was a few months older than Hubert, He possessed the beauty of his mother, with the dark, hidden nature of his father. He was stubborn, morose, and quarrelsome. He abounded in bad qualities, but if there was one which excelled another, it was cunning and duplicity. These were so combined as really to form but one. Had he been a man and termed *Jesuitical*, in the Protestant sense, that term would have aptly described him. Now Hubert was not perfect more than other children, but, compared to Thornton Rush, he was a little saint. His organ of combativeness frequently waged stern conflicts with his bump of reverence. His sense of right was keen as his sensitiveness against wrong and falsehood. He was, like his mother, frank and open as the day, generous, disinterested, and unselfish.

What should happen, then, when these two natures came together? What but thunder and lightning, as when two clouds meet?

Duncan Lisle thought about this as he saw his boy borne away from him, and he resolved to go over for him very soon after dinner. He arrived just in time to rescue him, bruised and bleeding, from the fists and fury of Thornton Rush. The quarrel had commenced in this way: Thornton had asserted that everything at Thornton Hall was his; Hubert had nothing. Hubert admitted as much, insisting, however, that all at Kennons was his.

"No such thing," denied Thornton. "Everything at Kennons

is your father's; you have nothing."

"Well," said the other, "so everything at Thornton Hall is your mother's, and not yours."

"No such thing. I am the master of Thornton Hall. My father is dead, sir."

"Yes, I know that."

"You know that! And is that all you can say? Say that I am master of Thornton Hall, and that you are nobody but Hubert Lisle," said Thornton, intent upon a quarrel.

"I shall say no such thing."

"But you will, sir, and I can make you. I am stronger than you are, and I have bigger fists. Look here, aren't you afraid?" shaking his clenched fist in the other's face.

"No, I am *not* afraid," spoke Hubert boldly, striving to grapple with his stronger foe.

So engaged were the boys, they heard not the approach of Mr. Lisle, till, having dismounted from his horse, he seized Thornton by the collar and flung him afar, as he would have done a wild cat.

Mrs. Rush, who had seen the whole from the window, and enjoyed it immensely, now thought it worth while to come upon the scene.

"What does all this mean?" as if just surprised. "Thornton Rush, you will be punished for this. Have you no better manners than to treat your young visitor in that way? Really, Mr. Lisle, I am truly distressed, and offer you a thousand apologies. Please do not take Hubert home in that condition; bring him to the kitchen and let Dinah bathe his face and hands. How unfortunate this should have occurred!"

Mr. Lisle complied, and waited until his boy was brought to him in a more presentable condition; then he went away, very wroth indeed in heart, but outwardly calm and composed.

CHAPTER X

"A DREAM WHICH WAS NOT ALL A DREAM"

As the missionary journeyed northward, his mind emerged from the gloom of the last few days. It naturally turned upon the young girl who was so soon to become his bride, and in this connection life began again to assume its rose-tints of old, and he was led to wonder how it was he had so given way to grief and sadness. In recalling the trials and disadvantages to which his young bride would be exposed at the mission, a bright thought occurred to him. An American housekeeper would be invaluable, and Miss Toothaker arose before him. She would no doubt prove an excellent manager, and she was so unprepossessing in every way, she would be unlikely to be appropriated by any widowed missionary. It has been seen already that for Philip St. Leger to think and to act were but quick, consecutive steps; it was so in this case. Upon his return to Troy he called upon Madame X—and explained his wishes. Miss Toothaker was consulted, and accepted his proposition at once; she would be on missionary ground at all events. True, she was conditionally engaged to marry a Mr. Freeman Clarke, who was an itinerant preacher. She had insisted that he should become a missionary. He had consented to go as missionary to the Western frontiers. This did not meet Miss Toothaker's views; foreign missionary or nothing. Mr. Clarke's conscience did not send him to any

Booriooboolah Gha, he said.

The engagement had been for some time in this state of contention, when the proposal of going to Turkey as "assistant" put an end to it.

Miss Arethusa retired to her room triumphantly, and exultingly wrote to her lover the facts in the case—except that she left him to infer that she was going to Turkey, as she had always wished, a missionary's wife.

Now that Mr. Freeman Clarke's "blessing had taken its flight," it all at once assumed that brightness of which the poet speaks. He would have argued and urged, even consented to have gone to the ends of the earth, but he saw from his lady's letter it was too late. He solaced himself somewhat by replying to her dolorously, hoping that she might perceive his heart was broken and be sorry. He closed loftily by saying: "You advise me, my dear Arethusa—allow me to call you thus for the last time—to find a heart worthier and better. It was unkind in you to urge upon me an impossibility. None but Napoleon ever scorned the word impossible."

Whether Mr. Freeman Clarke derived his inspiration for the itineracy from his lady-love is not for us to decide; this much is certain: from the day the "Atlantic" sailed for the Old World with Miss Toothaker on board his zeal flagged, and soon gave out altogether. His love for souls settled down upon one Annette Jones, the plain daughter of a plain farmer, whom he married, and lived happily enough with upon a small, rocky farm in the State of Vermont. In times of "revival," he became an "exhorter," and very fervent in prayer. Upon one occasion he soared to such a pitch as to cry out frantically: "O Lord, come down upon us now, come down now through the roof, *and I will pay for the shingles*."[A]

There were two or three people present who thought such an address to the Supreme Being blasphemous and frightful, but the rest of the crowd cried, "Amen."

In due time our missionaries found themselves at the house of Dr. Adams. The doctor was rejoiced to have back Minerva again, for he declared nothing had gone on rightly since her departure.

Although Philip was well pleased with his second wife, he forgot not his first. On the evening of his arrival he went out to visit her grave. As he stood there mournful and silent, a light step approached, and Emily's hand clasped his own.

"Is it *her* grave?" she asked softly.

"Yes. You would not have me quite forget Della, would you?" he asked, doubtfully.

"O, no, but I would remember her with you. I would stand here by her grave with you, and offer up my prayers with yours that she may look down upon us in love and blessing. I would not seek to drive her memory from your heart. I do not consider that I have usurped her place. I would have a place alongside of hers—if I am worthy, Philip." She added the last words in a whisper, and doubtingly.

For the first time Philip perceived what a treasure he had won, and how worthy a successor to his first love. He looked down in her tearful eyes lovingly.

"Della in heaven and Emily on earth—as one I love you," he said, fervently.

On the following day Philip took his bride out to view the wonders of the city. They invited Miss Toothaker to accompany them, but were by no means regretful that she declined. They little dreamed what was going on in their absence. Suffice to say, when, after a few days of rest, they began to make ready for departure, their "assistant" displayed not her accustomed zeal and alacrity. This was accounted for on the last morning of their stay.

Without warning or preliminaries, immediately after prayers, in fact, upon rising from his knees, Dr. Adams walked up to the blushing Miss Toothaker, and taking her happy hand, led her to the far end of the room, placing himself and her in position.

"Before you leave, Mr. St. Leger, you will, if you please, do us the favor"—(bowing low and smiling mellifluously) "you see how it is, sir, and what we wish of you." The Doctor stammered, and was bashful, although such a veteran in the service.

The bride elect held her head very erect; the red spots in her cheeks glowed like double peonies; her two thin curls, done in oil for the occasion, hung straight and stiff like pendant icicles nigrescent; her sparkling black eyes looked apparently into vacuity, while they were really beholding the acme of all her hopes. She was thinking in that supreme moment of her life how very providential it was that she had thrown overboard Mr. Freeman Clarke. Whether he was picked up or whether the sharks devoured him, it occurred not to her to care. That she was about to become the fourth wife of the Rev. Dr. Adams, foreign missionary at the Capitol city of Turkey, was sufficient glory; she could have afforded to quench the hopes, and tread upon the hearts of a dozen such as that itinerant preacher. She had reserved herself for a grand calling, her life would be written in a book, and *her* name too, along with the Judsons, the Newells, the Deans, would inspire Sunday school scholars with zeal for missionary life unto the end of time.

But we are keeping them waiting.

Philip, always master of the situation, choked down his indignation and spoke the words, "for better—for worse." His prayer was brief and dry, without one bit of heart or spirit, but maybe it answered the purpose.

The Doctor, after the tying of the knot, did condescend to thank Philip for his kindness in bringing him over a wife. Philip replied with truthfulness that he merited no thanks.

And after all, once started again upon their inland journey, both Philip and his wife regretted not the absence of Arethusa. They had endured her company for sake of the advantage she was to prove to them in the future; they now fully realized how much she had been in their way.

Philip's respect for the Doctor sensibly diminished. If he could endure Miss Arethusa for the the rest of his life, his taste was abominable. *De gustibus non disputandum est*; with this familiar reflection, Philip turned to a subject more agreeable.

Thus had Arethusa's life-long dream of becoming a missionary's wife proved neither illusive nor vain; and she had dropped the Toothaker.

[Footnote A: A fact.]

CHAPTER XI

ALTHEA'S GUARDIANS

The little Althea then, who is our heroine, when we shall
come to her, had been entrusted, somewhat unwillingly, to
her aunt, Juliet St. Leger Temple; Juliet never wrote her
name only in full, as above. She was proud of her maiden
name. St. Leger was romantic, high-sounding, aristocratic.
Temple—well, Temple had been well enough in the early
days of her courtship. She thought she loved John Temple so
very profoundly that she would have married him even if he
went by Smith or Jones. She had read Charlotte Temple, and
she knew people by that name of great respectability; but
since her marriage, she had discovered, on the same street
with her, a family of Temples who were snobbish and
vulgar. This put her out of conceit with her husband's name.
John Temple! so almost the same as James Temple, only a
few squares below. Who was to distinguish her, Mrs. Juliet
St. Leger Temple, from the fat, dowdyish, over-dressed,
gaudy Mrs. Temple, who wore a wig, and whose eyes
squinted? Who, she questioned, when both went by the name
of Mrs. J. Temple, of M—street? Her early married life was
clouded by this one grievance. She had still another; her
husband was a Roman Catholic, and would not go with her
to St. Mark's Church. True, she had known him to be a
Catholic when she married him; but she had *not* known or

dreamed that these Catholics were so set and obstinate in their religion. He had been so reticent upon the subject that she had supposed him quite indifferent. Once married, she could convert him; O, that would be a very easy matter. He need go to St. Mark's but once to be so delighted that he would wish to go there ever after. She had consented to be married first by the priest in order that John Temple might see the delightful difference between being married by Father Duffy at low Mass in the early morning, while fashionables were still folding their hands in slumber, and being married five hours after by the elegant Dr. Browne, assisted by the Rev. Drs. Knickerbocker and Breck—with a brilliant group of brides-maids and groomsmen, and only the very *elite* of fashion, full-dressed and perfumed, in attendance.

"I hope he will be captivated now; and that here will ooze out the last gasp of his love for the religion of St. Patrick," the young bride had said mentally.

But neither Dr. Browne, nor his beaming assistants, nor all the splendor of St. Mark's made upon John Temple the least apparent impression.

The Sunday following the marriage witnessed quite a contention.

"And you say this positively, John, that you will not go with me to St. Mark's, and on the very first Sunday, too?" cried Juliet, incredulous. "I have told you all along that I would not go to your church," replied John.

"But what possible harm could there be in your going just this once? Any other man in the world would be proud to go with me in all my beautiful bridal array. I assure you there is not another wardrobe in the city so *recherche* as mine. You yourself said you never saw such a love of a hat, and my point-lace might be the pride of a princess. But, John, if you would only go, I would be more proud of you than even anything and all of my elegant dress. Now, John, dear, please say yes," and she laid her hand on his arm, and looked up, as she vainly hoped, irresistibly in his face.

But John shook off her hand impatiently, not deigning even to respond to her look.

"Silence gives consent, and you will go," she said.

"Have I not told you once, twice, and thrice that I cannot go with you?"

"O, John, but I did not think you in such terrible earnest, and you are not, I am sure. I thought you loved me so well you would do anything to please me. Come now, just this once, this first Sunday after our marriage. Think how it will look, and what will people say to see me walk into church all alone—and our pew is far up in front?"

"Is it for the looks of the thing and for what people will say that you go to church?" asked the husband, gravely.

"No, of course not; but then we must have some regard for the speech of people, and how it will look for you to go off to one church and your wife to another."

"Would you care to go with me, Juliet?"

"With you? To St. Patrick's? With all the Bridgets and Pats and Mikes of the city? Do you think I could stoop so low? O, John Temple, you insult me!" and the young wife burst into indignant tears.

John hurried to her with his handkerchief to wipe her eyes.

She thrust it away, declaring there was something about a gentleman's handkerchief that made it abominable.

"Well, don't cry, dear," urged John, soothingly.

"It's all the comfort left me," sobbed Juliet.

"I simply followed your example," continued the husband. "You invited me to your church, and I invited you to mine, that, as you said, we might go together. I had no idea of urging you to go if it would be disagreeable to you."

"There's a vast difference. If you go to St. Mark's you are among elegant people. Every one's dress is in the height of fashion. You see nothing low or vulgar. There is nothing to offend the senses. The very thought of my going to St. Patrick's!" and the lady cast up her eyes as if she were about to faint or to implore Heaven to save her from such a horror.

"But you associate in society with the McCaffreys, the Dempseys, and the Blakes, and many others of the congregation of St. Patrick."

"O, well, they probably started up from nothing, and are used to it; they don't know any difference. But for me—a St. Leger! O, John, if you love me, don't ever mention such a thing again; and if you love me, John, a half or quarter as I love you, you will go with me to St. Mark's. I will not go without you, and I shall cry myself into a dreadful headache, and you can refuse me and see me suffer so when we've been married but five days! O dear, dear, I thought I was going to marry a man who would love me so well he would do everything in the world to please me, and now here it is!" and Juliet fairly shook with sobs.

John Temple was a very matter-of-fact man; quite the

reverse of his wife in every respect. The wonder is how such opposites became attracted. He understood very little of women's ways, and became fearful that his young bride was on the borders of distraction. He felt himself justified in remaining absent from Mass, and as he persevered in his resolution of not accompanying Juliet to St. Mark's, both remained at home, where more of clouds than sunshine reigned.

More than once during this scene John Temple was on the point of yielding. Where was the harm after all? and it would be a pleasure to gratify Juliet. But he remembered the promise he had made to himself and his God, that, in marrying a Protestant wife, he would still keep aloof from the Protestant Church. This promise kept him true. If once would have answered, he might have gone once; but after that the battle would have to be fought over again; the victory might be made complete in the beginning.

The next day, while Mr. Temple was at his place of business, Juliet, feeling herself very much injured, visited her rector, Dr. Browne. She told him the whole story in her tragic way, including the insulting proposal for her to go to St. Patrick's. She wished Dr. Browne would contrive some way by which her her husband might be brought to terms.

Dr. Browne smiled.

"You will remember, Mrs. Temple," he said, "that your friends all warned you in this matter of your marriage. It is so impossible for a Catholic to become anything else, that it has become an adage, 'Once a Catholic, always a Catholic.' Do not expect your husband to change; the leopard might as well be expected to change his spots. Ephraim is joined to his idols; let him alone. Let him go to his church, and you to yours. It is not pleasant, but must be accepted as one of the conditions of your marriage. Neither let it create trouble between you. Avoid religious subjects. But as he will undoubtedly cling to his Church, so must you to yours. Do not be prevailed upon to go with him; remain upon that point firm as himself."

Thereafter Juliet concluded she had better make the best of it, and by-and-bye it had ceased to become the "skeleton in the house," as at first.

Had Juliet been less exacting and less demonstrative in her affection, she would have made her husband a happier man. Coming home one day he found her crying, as if her heart would break. To his eager inquiries as to the cause, she replied, hysterically:

"You don't love me, John, and I am the most unhappy woman in the world."

"Don't love you! What has put such a notion as that in your head?"

"You know you don't, John; that is enough."

"But if I tell you I do?"

"That is just what you never do tell me; that is what makes me so miserable."

"Am I unkind to you? What have I done that you complain of?"

"You don't tell me every day that you love me."

"Bless me! You are not expecting me to repeat that over every day? Is not once enough for all? Did I not prove it beyond all words by marrying you?"

"I never expected our honeymoon to wane. If you calculated to settle down at once into sober old married people, I did not, nor will I. I wish we had never got married, and always stayed lovers; that was ever so much nicer. Don't you say your *Ave Maria* every day?"

"I do," answered John, "or rather I used to," failing to perceive what connection this question could have with the subject.

"Well, then, why do you do that? Why don't you say it once for all and have done with it, as you say of your love for me? But no, all your devotion must be given to a woman that lived thousands of years ago! You think more of her picture than of your own wife! This is what one gets by marrying a Catholic!"

Juliet's temper was fast overcoming her grief.

John Temple was agitated by a variety of emotions. He looked at his wife, who had re-buried her face in the sofa cushions, and thus addressed her, inaudibly:

"You foolish, little simpleton! you ignorant little heretic!— destitute both of religion and common sense. Good Heavens, what a wife! Jealous of Mary, our Mother in Heaven! O, Holy Mary in Heaven, pray for her."

The dinner-bell rang.

"Come, Juliet," said her husband, kindly, "let us go to dinner; I am hungry as a bear."

"You can go; I have no appetite, I never care to eat again as long as I live," came out dismally from the depths of the pillows.

John ate a hearty dinner, when, failing to conciliate his wife, he went to his office. No sooner had the hall-door closed on him than Juliet arose out of her sackcloth and ashes, bathed her face, arranged her hair, and proceeding to the dining-room, so far forgot her intention of never eating again as to surprise the cook by her greediness. She then dressed, ordered her carriage, and was driven to her mother's.

To this mother, who was a confirmed invalid, and confined to the house, Juliet poured out the exaggerated tale of her grievances. It was not enough that her husband was a Catholic; he was also heartless, stoical, unsympathizing, and unloving.

Mrs. St. Leger listened silently to the end. At the conclusion she flew into a rage.

"You shall go back to him no more," she exclaimed. "You see now the folly of your persisting in marrying him. He was beneath you in every respect. But you shall not live with him. My daughter shall not be treated disdainfully by John Temple, an Irishman and a Catholic. I will send for my lawyer and have divorce papers drawn at once. Ring for Richard."

"But, mamma—I—I—I never thought of getting a divorce. I love my husband. It is because I love him so well that I feel so bad if—if—"

"Juliet, you are a goose," interrupted the irritated parent; "if you are so fond of your husband, what are you here for with your complaints? If you are bound to live with him, why, live with him, and hold your tongue. When it comes that you are willing to separate and get a divorce, then come to me, but not till then."

Juliet returned to her home a wiser woman. The very thought of separation from her husband was distracting. What was mother or sister compared to him? She had really no doubt of his affection, and it suddenly flashed upon her mind that such scenes as she had just gotten up, if frequently repeated, might have a tendency to alienate him. She would make it all up; she would tell him how sorry she was; she would be so glad to see him; he *should* love her, even though he did not tell her so.

John came home that night wondering if he should find his wife's face still hidden in the cushions, her hair standing out in a thousand dishevelled threads. It was not a pleasant picture. Yet it *was* a pleasant picture that met him at the door. Juliet was all smiles, blooms and roses. There was joy in her eyes, and gladness in her tones. Never had she looked quite so beautiful to John Temple—even when first her beauty won him. It was such a surprise! What wonder he committed the folly—but no matter. Juliet learned a lesson to her advantage. Tears and upbraidings had failed to move him. A happy face, smiles, charming toilettes, joy at his coming had brought out those expressions which demands had failed to elicit.

Juliet was not satisfied yet. She had to tell him how shocked she had been at the mere thought of losing him. John opened his eyes, and felt considerably hurt as she detailed the visit to her mother, and that mother's proposition for a divorce. For Juliet touched very lightly upon her own fault of having made outrageous complaints against him. Nevertheless he felt convinced of the facts, knowing Juliet had gone there with unkindness in her heart. By his repeated questionings she admitted all, but he fully forgave her, considering the good results of her thoughtless action.

On the day following this domestic breeze and subsequent calm, Philip St. Leger had arrived from the Orient. Two months previously they had been apprised of his coming. A family conclave had been held, at which it had been decided that to Juliet should Philip's child be consigned; for reasons already explained by Philip to Duncan Lisle.

Juliet had now been married six months. She was twenty-five years of age; old enough to have exhibited more sense and discretion than we have seen her to do. She was, however, one of those who will be childish as long as they live. Her faults and delinquencies were due more to improper training than to natural defects. With such characters is hope of reformation.

Juliet was delighted with the child, which was just commencing to walk, and could say a few words. She had the dark eyes and hair, and creamy complexion of the St. Legers.

Juliet had been, even among girls, distinguished for her love of dolls. To make dresses and hats for her troop of a dozen had formed one of the chief pleasures of her childhood, continued far up into youth.

In Althea she saw the quintessence of all dolls. For her she could embroider, ruffle, and tuck; search the city over for the daintiest of baby shoes and the showiest of infant hats. Althea should have a nurse, and a carriage, and a poodle dog. Santa Claus should not only give her his choicest gifts at Christmas but should shower down toys every day in the year. After a little, in another year, she would take her with her to St. Mark's, where she should attract all eyes by her dress and beauty.

That Althea had a soul to be trained, carefully guided and directed to God, entered not into the calculations of this giddy, superficial woman.

CHAPTER XII

THE CHRISTENING

A year afterward came little Johnny into the house of the Temples. Words altogether fail to do justice to the mother's pride and joy.

Leonora, who wore proudly her husband's grand name of Van Rensaleer, looked down on the Temples; nevertheless, as a duty, she called to congratulate them upon the birth of a son.

"Yes, a fine babe," she replied to the father's questioning look of admiration. "A nice baby, I dare say," she said in answer to Juliet's glowing extolations, finished by a "do you not think so?" "But all babies look alike to me," she added. "I fail to see the charm, I prefer my poodle."

"Sour grapes," returned Juliet, her eyes flashing.

"Sweet grapes, my dear," said her sister, softly. "Well, I wish you much joy, and may the child prove a blessing to you."

Then came Estelle. She was Mrs. Lang. She had married an Englishman, and would have gotten along comfortably had she not been "worried to death" with "those children." Hugh was now four years old, the twins two and a-half, and Robby in his eleventh month. Four boys, and they kept the house in commotion from one year's end to another.

To Juliet's joyful outbursts Estelle answered: "O, it is all very well just now; I know all about it; but wait until you have four! Why, I cannot get from the sound of their noise; it rings in my ears now. There isn't a moment when I am not on the keen jump, expecting some limb to be broken, some eye to be put out, or some dreadful disease to come around. I dread the warm season on account of its summer-complaints; and the cold for its croups, scarlet fevers, measles, and whooping cough. I warn you, Juliet, you are seeing your happiest days." And Estelle, with a weary look and dreary tone, took her departure for her luxurious, but uproarious home.

"What are *you* going to do with the baby?" asked Mr. Temple of the little Althea.

"I yock it," she answered, placing her hand upon her own small crib, rocking it to and fro.

The young mother, excited and nervous, would not heed the Doctor's cautions to keep herself quiet. Like many another foolish person, she thought she knew better than any physician could tell her. As a result of her indiscretion, she was attacked with a long and dangerous illness, which had nearly proved fatal.

Upon her recovery, Johnny was three months old; and Juliet began to talk about having him baptized. The first time she went out to drive she purchased the finest christening robe she could find. Nothing was too expensive for such an occasion. For herself also she obtained an entirely new outfit. If John could only be induced to go to the christening! Possibly he might; she would make one more effort.

One day when he came home at noon she met him smilingly at the door.

"John, come with me a minute," she said, and led the way up the winding stairway, into the finest chamber. The bed and every article of furniture was made to do duty in supporting beautiful and costly fabrics.

"What! another wedding to take place?" exclaimed John.

"The christening of our only child, my dear. See, everything is ready; just look at this elegant robe, fit for a king's son, but only worthy of our dear boy. O John, I have only one drawback to all my happiness—if you would only go with us to St. Mark's!"

"Juliet, why do you wish our child to be baptized?" inquired John.

"If you please, say *christened*. Why, is it not customary? Do not everybody who are any thing take their children to the church? Indeed, it is a very grand occasion; I suppose little innocent children are not admitted at St. Patrick's?"

"On the contrary, every Catholic child is baptized, even at the most tender age; but, Juliet, the Catholic mother gives not all her mind to the child's costly apparel; that is of little consequence compared to devoting the child to God."

"That is not the question," spoke Juliet, impatiently. "Will you, or will you not go with us to St. Mark's?"

"Juliet, I have something I should tell you. Our child has been baptized. I took him myself to the house of Father Duffy several weeks ago."

"You did? How dared you?" cried Juliet, angrily.

"I had the same right to take him to Father Duffy as have you to take him to Dr. Browne. You were very ill at the time; I did not like to wait."

"It doesn't matter at all," cried Juliet, recovering herself, "I will take him to St. Mark's just the same."

"You should inform Dr. Browne, however, that the child has been already baptized."

"*He* will not think he has been baptized; but I will tell him, and let him know how unfairly you have dealt with me."

Juliet did not know what her husband was aware of, that Dr. Browne, or any Episcopal clergyman, would consider baptism at the hands of a Catholic priest as true and valid.

The Sunday appointed for the christening drew near. On the Saturday preceding, Juliet called on Dr. Browne. Having largely expatiated upon her happy anticipations of the morrow, she proceeded to relate to the rector the march her husband had stolen upon her.

"And do you not know, Mrs. Temple," said the doctor, surprised, "that, if your child has been baptized by Father Duffy, that is sufficient? There is no need for our ceremony to-morrow," and the rector saw in imagination a handsome fee that failed to reach his grasp.

"Is it possible," cried Juliet, disappointed and grieved to the heart, "that you consider baptism in the Catholic Church of any worth whatsoever?"

"Most assuredly we do," answered the doctor.

"But I thought they were idolaters and heathens. How can heathens baptize?"

"The Romish was the first Apostolic Church; after many years it imbibed errors and became corrupt. The Church of which we are members, which should really be termed Catholic and not Episcopal, came out from her, retaining her truth, rejecting her errors and superstitions. We maintain that the Church of Christ must be Apostolic, therefore are compelled to admit that to have been the true Church from which we sprang. We are really a branch of the Romish Church, unpalatable as it may be to some of us."

Had Juliet given attention to the rector's theology, she would have remarked that it was giving the Romish Church too much credit. But for her his words fell idly; she was intent on having her baby christened at St. Mark's.

"But, Dr. Browne, nobody knows my baby has been baptized. Cannot the christening go on just the same?"

"By no means," spoke the clergyman, decidedly. "It is contrary to custom, and to the laws of the Church."

Juliet went home sick at heart. So many preparations, and all for nothing; so many hopes and dreams, and all blown up like bubbles. In her grief and confusion the complicated question as to whether her child were a Catholic or an Episcopalian did not intrude itself.

She did stop to marvel, however, as to whether her husband had given more than one name to the baby. She had intended his second name should be St. Leger. But her husband was so absent-minded, she presumed to say that he had forgotten all about it. Upon questioning him he looked up somewhat confused.

"I had indeed forgotten your intention. I do remember now of having heard you speak of St. Leger; I do remember."

"So you had him christened without a middle name, plain John Temple! I wonder you didn't go to the length of giving him your own name in full, John Patrick Temple!"

"That I did do, my dear; it was my father's name, and I never thought but what it had been all settled between us."

This was too much for Juliet's patience, already tried. She stamped her feet, wrung her hands, and cried aloud despairingly.

When, at length, able to articulate, she poured upon John Temple's ears such a shower of words as must have refreshed the very springs of his nature. She concluded thus:

"You are the most set, stupid, obstinate man in this world, and selfish too. It was not enough that I should have given him your old-fashioned, homely, plain name of John, when Alphonsus, Adolphus, or Rinaldo would have suited me so much better, but you must put in that low, vulgar, most hateful of all names—Patrick! A Patrick in our own house, for our only child! By and bye, he will be going by the name of Pat. *My* child—the son of a St. Leger—baptized by a Catholic priest and called Pat, just like the dozen other infant nobodies he had baptized the same day, no doubt. Nothing to distinguish him from the vulgar herd—a paddy among paddies! O John Temple, I wish I had never seen your face and eyes!"

John Temple seized hurriedly his hat, and without a word went out from the presence of his wife. To say that he was not angry would be untrue. Above his anger, however, swelled emotions of surprise and wonder. Surprise and wonder that the beautiful Juliet St. Leger, during six months of intimate courtship, so successfully could have veiled, under constant guise of amiability, the weak, pettish nature which she was now so often exhibiting.

Of a truth, he had been simple enough to become attracted by her exceeding beauty of face and figure; but these accidents would never have held a man of his sterling sense and uprightness had he not been led to believe it associated with a corresponding beauty of mind and disposition.

For a brief while this strong man yielded to an overwhelming sense of loss and regret. The memory of his excellent mother came back, by comparison, to increase his painful confusion.

"My mother, my good mother," he sighed, "noblest and best of Christian women, for me you died one year too soon. You at least would have read aright the heart of Juliet. Sainted mother, for thy sake, for all our sakes, I will do well by Juliet. Since it is as it is, God help me, I will not fail."

And Juliet, after the anger had cooled in her heart, and the flush died out somewhat in her cheek, mused thus:

"Was ever another such man as John Temple since the days of Job the patient? There is no satisfaction in scolding him. Not a word will he say, but march off dignified as any Lord Admiral. A grand way that is of heaping coals on my head. I wish I could learn to bite my tongue, as I know he does his. I am really afraid he will come to disrespect and despise me. Why can not I mend my ways? But it was aggravating, wasn't it, Johnnie," turning to his babyship, "to give mamma's darling a very, very horrible name, and have water poured on his sweet little head by a naughty, wicked, Irish Romish priest. Yes, that it was, Johnnie dear, and we won't stand it, will we, Johnnie darling?"

Johnnie signified his concurrence of sentiment by a masterly plunge of his fat fingers into his precious mamma's curls, which entanglement caused a rapid "change to come o'er the spirit of her dream."

The anticipated grand Sunday was spent at home by Juliet, in her own room. The furniture in the best chamber was still graced by her unappropriated apparel. The christening robe, heavy with embroidery, hung as if for a crime from its temporary gallows. Juliet stepped in, viewing them but an instant, then withdrew, locking the door behind her. Had she seen the seven hanging heads of Bluebeard's decapitated wives, she would not have been more pained. She returned to her room to weep over her poor baby, which she regarded as a martyr. Yes, ill-treated had he been, contemptuously treated; she could have no more pride in him: henceforth he would be to her an object of pity.

Going and returning from Mass that morning, John Temple began to inquire if he had not indeed rather wronged his wife, in giving that name to the child, which he knew to be so repugnant to her taste. He would not have liked his child to be called Luther or Calvin. He had been thoughtless and stupid to be sure. Reaching home, he sought Juliet. He found her in her oldest wrapper, her face red with weeping, her hair frightfully unkempt.

"Juliet," he began, kindly, "I would never have given Johnnie that name—"

"But you did give it to him," interrupted Juliet.

"I did; but giving very little heed to the name. You were very dangerously sick. The physician declared you could not live six hours, unless change took place for the better. The child had been ailing. I thought of baptism for both of you—to the child it could be given. I ordered a carriage, put the nurse and child in and drove to Father Duffy's. I had not thought of the name until asked by the priest. In the confusion of the moment I gave it as I did. I should not have insisted on the name had you been with me. It should have been anything you wished. When he becomes old enough to be confirmed the name can be changed."

"His name shall never be written with a P. It shall be written J. St. Leger Temple. I will get Dr. Browne to put it upon the Registry. Does Father Duffy record names too?"

Mr. Temple replying in the affirmative, the young mother became seized with another spasm of terror.

"Then Father Duffy believes he has got that child in the Catholic Church, I suppose! O, what a fearful piece of work you have made of it! No doubt, like King Solomon, he will be for dividing the child, that he may get at least half its soul for purgatory. And if I had died, you would have brought up dear little Johnnie a Catholic! Your great hurry for his baptism shows it. That is the regard you would have shown for my memory! But I am not dead yet; and while I live, the child goes with me to St Mark's. I will still do all *I* can to bring him up respectably."

A day or two after appeared in the city a foreign songstress who was setting the whole world mad. John Temple took his wife to hear her. She threw off, as they had been a bundle of straw, all these troubles that had so crazed her. She unlocked the best chamber, went in, and came out looking beautiful as when a bride. Among her friends again she appeared as if no cloud of sorrow had ever darkened her life.

John Temple recognized his wife again. By these repeated scenes of sunshine and storm, he learned to rejoice in the one, and to remain undisturbed in the other; against the exuberance of one to present the parasol of calmness, and the umbrella of patience to ward off descending floods.

Three years later, one winter's evening at tea, the dining-room servant informed John, upon his inquiring for her mistress, that that lady wished to see him in the best chamber. He had not seen her since early in the morning. At dinner he had been told that she was lying down, and wished not to be disturbed. Having hurried through his tea, he repaired to the room designated. The first object that met his view was very large Mrs. Biggs overflowing the arm-chair, with a roll of white flannel in her lap, over which Althea and Johnny were absorbingly bending.

"We've got a baby, papa!" "Mrs. Biggs has brought us a baby!" cried out the children simultaneously.

Mr. Temple evinced the greatest surprise, of course, but walked straight up to his wife. She smiled upon him mischievously, saying:

"You are surprised to find me here and not in our own room?"

When the perplexed husband had nodded his head, the wife continued:

"I wished to be up-stairs for two reasons: the second is because they say it is a sign that the child who beholds the light for the first time above stairs will be surely rich; and the first, because—because—O, John, I have stolen a march on *you* this time—I wanted Dr. Browne to be sent for and the christening over with before you should know there was a baby in the house. Little Flora Isabella Ernestine has been already christened;" and the wife's eyes were full of triumph.

"All right," replied John Temple, smiling grimly; and he was fain to kiss his wife, and to cast a satisfied glance at the "sole daughter of his house and heart," which was so royally blessed with abundance of name. In his view the child was not yet baptized, and at a convenient season he would take it to Father Duffy; but he would not trouble his wife by disclosing this intention.

CHAPTER XIII

NEW MISTRESS AT KENNONS

"When a woman will, she will, you may depend on't,
When she won't, she won't, and there's an end on't."

Mrs. Jerusha Thornton Rush, from the time of Ellice's death, had firmly resolved on marrying Duncan Lisle. He, on the other hand, had firmly resolved never to allow that scheming widow to supplant his lost wife.

Whether her will was stronger than his, or whether he changed his mind, it matters not; at the end of three years Mrs. Rush had carried her point and become Mrs. Lisle—one of the incomprehensibilities which may be left without comment.

She had struggled so long and doubtfully for the prize, that, by the time she had won it, she was disposed to undervalue and despise it.

"I will make him feel in his turn, when in my power, how charming the sensation of being spitted or speared!" she had threatened, and she kept her word.

"I jist knowed it from de fust," declared Aunt Amy, sorrow

and anger in her tones, and the Indian expression assuming mastery in her face. "Somehow I jist felt it all over me dat dat woman would come aroun' massa and jes make him marry her. She's 'witched him; she's gin him love-potions, I make no doubt; and I 'spec's"—here she lowered her voice to a whisper—"I 'spec's she's sold herself to de debil to make him help her. Nuthin' else could ever 'duced Massa Duncan to marry such a—such a crocodile. He'll never be sorry but onc't, and 'dats all his life."

"Der's an end to all our 'joyment," sighed Chloe, grown more weighty in flesh; "de Lord knows what's going to become of us—an' all her host o' bad niggers mixin' in wid our'n, and she domineerin' ober eberyting. O, it's an orful bad day for us, sure! An', then, that hateful boy o' her'n—he's worse 'an pizen, notstan'ing his slick, ile-y ways—'tween him an' her we'll stan' mighty slim chance. She bad's bad can be, an' he worse."

China shed tears silently over her needle, giving now and then a groan. She, too, was haunted by a presentiment that her happy days were over. For her, Miss Rusha, as all the servants called her, had ever evinced unconcealed dislike, for the very reason, it would seem, that it irked her to behold any person in peace and contentment. She especially hated meek, gentle, uncomplaining people, and loved to render them uncomfortable. And China, Ellice's favorite house-servant, was so good, gentle, and obedient, that her former mistress had seldom found fault with her.

Mr. Lisle, immediately after his marriage, had taken his bride North on a visit to the principal cities, intending to call upon the Temples, to make acquaintance with his loved sister's child.

His stay at this latter place was short indeed, for Miss Rusha, presuming to find fault with Juliet's mode of training, or rather of indulging Althea, had provoked the latter lady's ire to such a degree as to render any further tarrying out of the question. For some reason or other, Mrs. Lisle would have persuaded her husband to make an effort for gaining the guardianship of his niece. This, however, he peremptorily refused to do, although he became greatly attached to the child, who was lovely and winning to a remarkable degree.

Upon the return to Kennons of the newly-married people, a tutor was secured for the two boys, Thornton and Hubert. It was soon found, however, that Kennons was not large enough for them both; that they could not study peaceably in the same room, nor, without a quarrel, at least in words, exercise upon the same grounds. The tutor was overwearied with incessant struggles to keep the two from variance. He advised that one should be sent away, or, if both should be sent, they should go to different points of the compass. Mrs. Lisle would not consent for her only child to go away from her; as to Thornton, he declared he would not be sent away to school. Hubert was more willing, at home his life was a misery on account of Thornton and his mother; any other place would be preferable, thought this motherless boy of eleven years. He was accordingly sent to a Northern school, where, with intervals of vacation, he spent the next eight years of his life.

The servants at Kennons had not been mistaken in their calculations. The new mistress sowed divisions and discord with a lavish hand. Duncan was annoyed with complaints against this and that one, until his patience gave way, and he plainly told his wife that he would not listen to them; that his servants were uncommonly good until she had come in the midst of them. Greatly exasperated at this, she treated them still more harshly. She placed over them her own servants, not out of love for them, but to humiliate those who had been the faithful servants and friends of her hated rival, Ellice.

China was the first victim. She was too ladylike in her deportment, too quiet and silent in her ways. She was ousted from her low rocker and favorite window, deprived of her needle, which had in some sort become a life-companion, and made to do all sorts of drudgery; no settled work, but hurried from that, this, and the other; never knowing what was coming next—the hardest kind of work—slavery, indeed.

China endeavored to do faithfully all that she was bidden; sewing, however, was her trade; she knew how to do naught else well; she was consequently chidden and scolded from morning until night.

Mrs. Lisle's antipathy toward her grew every day more strong. She sought a cause for having her degraded from the rank of house-servant to field-hand. She had employed more than one fruitless stratagem.

China was very fond of oranges. Probably this taste had been cultivated by her former mistress, who, also, being very partial to the same fruit, often shared her stores with her favorite servant. Mrs. Lisle became aware of this. She placed some oranges in the drawer of her bureau, and, contrary to custom, ordered China to "set the room to rights."

Morning after morning the fault-finding mistress counted her oranges, and, to her disappointment, found not one missing.

On the fourth morning the fatal drawer was left slightly drawn. As China passed it with her duster the perfume caught her attention; she peeped within, and the gleam of the oranges tempted her vision; she gazed at them as did Eve at the apples; she took one in her hands, and thrust it to her nose; she said to herself, "My dear Miss Ellice would have given me some of these; Miss Rusha is too mean for human; perhaps she would never miss one; if she did, how was she to know who took it?" and thrusting the orange in her pocket, she finished hastily her work, went out of sight and sound, and feasted upon the coveted dainty. No sooner was it devoured than she repented heartily. The serpent had tempted her; she had yielded; now, when the mischief was done, he called her a fool, and promised her she should be discovered; he did not tell her how soon; and though China was filled with fears, she little dreamed that that very moment her relentless enemy was triumphing over her success.

"An orange has been stolen from my drawer," exclaimed Miss Rusha, severely, to the knot of servants summoned together by her order; "stolen without leave or license," reiterated the angry mistress, though, in truth, more secretly pleased than angry, "and I am bound to know who is the offender. A thief shall not remain in this house; and I here warn you all that she who proves to be the culprit shall be condemned to the fields."

The women and girls sidled about, grinning, ogling each other with swimming eyes. China, however, was an exception; she looked neither to the right nor left, but trembled, and was downcast. It flashed over her quick mind instantly that for her a trap had been deliberately laid, and she had stepped straight into it.

China had heretofore prided herself upon her truthfulness and honesty; to this she had been trained by the best of mistresses; and if there was aught on earth she despised it was a deceitful, thieving servant. O, how had she fallen!

Buried in her own painful emotions, China had not noticed that the question put to and denied by the others was now addressed to her.

"Do you not hear? Are you deaf and dumb, China, that you do not answer me? Speak, now! Did you, or did you not, steal this orange?"

Thus suddenly aroused from this painful reverie to confront the angered eyes of the mistress she both feared and hated, she hesitated, then said, in a low tone, but defiantly:

"*I did not.*"

At that moment China hated herself more than her mistress, and glanced helplessly around, as if for some fig-leaf beneath which to hide.

"You did not!" repeated the mistress slowly and with emphasis, fastening upon the poor girl her merciless eyes. "You say you did not; all the servants say they did not. We will see."

Mrs. Lisle produced a tiny paper from her pocket, and emptied its powdered contents into half a wine-glass of water; stirring the mixture, she gave a spoonful to each suspected person, and then ordered them to stand in a row in the back-yard.

This cruel woman watched to see the sable faces turned to a deathly yellow; ipecacuanha was a successful rack and torture. To all, however, but to China, did the consciousness of innocence afford alleviation. Fresh pieces of peel ejected from her stomach gave ample witness as to who had purloined the orange. All her companions were surprised, some grieved, some rejoiced; for

"Base Envy withers at another's joy,

And hates that excellence it cannot reach."

"It is well for pride to have a fall," said one.

"She thought herself so much better'n all the rest on us," quoth another.

"I allus thought she wa'nt no better'n she should be, for all her puttin' on such airs," spoke a third contemptuously.

"She won't find no rocking-chair, nor no time to sing love-songs, nor make herself bows and fine lady fixins out in de corn and 'bacco patch. Heigho!" crowed Dinah.

Amy's Indian eyes swam in tears, and she and the mighty Chloe cast pitiful glances at their disgraced companion.

"She never did it of her own 'cord," thought the shrewd Amy; "Miss Rusha jes threw on her her spell; she 'witched her as she did Massa; she made her go do it; she jes did now, so!"

"You will not enter the house again," said Mrs. Lisle to the proved culprit. "My Jane will bring your things from Aunt Amy's cabin, which she has allowed you to occupy—you are never to let me see you about the place again—never—or you will rue the day. I will see Mr. Fuller, the overseer, who will assign you a place. Now go, deceitful thief and liar—your punishment is but too mild."

China, in going out from the home of her master, would fain have gone around by the grave of Ellice. But, besides thinking she might be watched, she felt in her disgrace too unworthy to kneel upon that sacred soil.

So, scarcely able to hold herself upright, which she must needs do, in order to support her bundle upon her head, she walked wearily onward, from the fair white house of Kennons, down the well-worn path that led to the rude, unsightly cabins of the field-hands, still more rude.

She was still weak, and suffering from effects of the harsh emetic, and this, with her shame and sorrow at her crime, more than her banishment, rendered her hopeless and wretched.

Duncan Lisle was riding slowly homeward from a consultation with his overseer. Whose was that reeling, swaying figure in the path before him? Not China of pleasant face, of quiet speech and mien? No, and yes. What could it mean? What mortal sickness of mind or body had wrought such ghastly woe in the face but yesterday so placid?

"Are you China, or China's ghost?" questioned he, drawing rein as he came up to this favorite house-servant.

"You have said it, master Duncan; I am but the ghost of poor China," and the ponderous bundle dropped first to the horse's nose and then at his forefeet, while her face fell into her trembling hands, her tears flowing down through her fingers, the first that she had shed.

"Tell me all about it, China—but the sun is hot, come under the shade of this tree," and the master led the way to an umbrageous beech close by. There, still resting upon his horse, while China leaned against the enormous trunk, the story was told of the day's doings without exaggeration or extenuation.

Though it was a clear story of theft and falsehood, Duncan Lisle naturally took the same view of it as had the humble Amy. The master of Kennons had not been ignorant of his wife's systematic persecution of this inoffensive servant. He had more than once spoken to her on the subject—but finding he had but made the matter worse, ceased to interfere. Now, he suspected China to be the victim of a successful plot. His wife had made a bold move, and without his sanction. A more fiery man, yielding to indignation and to a sense of the injustice wrought, would have taken China home again, saying to his wife both by word and action, that he was still master in his own house, and of his own servants. But Duncan Lisle knew that life for China at the house was over. She had been long enough suffering incessant martyrdom under the heavy sway of the new mistress. Yes, it would be better for her to go away. He regarded her pityingly; then that emotion was quickly reflected from her to himself.

"*She* can go away—*she* can find happiness elsewhere. O, is there not somewhere in the wide world a place of beautiful peace?" groaned the unhappy man to himself, while his eyes wandered involuntarily toward the white column that gleamed in the sunlight nearly a mile distant. By an effort the master recovered himself.

"So she has sent you down to be with Bet, and Nan, and Kizzie, and Sam, Jake, Jim, and all those fellows? You can't live there a month. Would you like your freedom, China? Would you like to go to Richmond—you could get plenty of places, either as nurse or seamstress?"

"O, master Duncan, I should die if I had to leave Kennons"—for this first thought of complete separation from all she had known and loved was intolerable.

"You can try it then down yonder. I will ride down to-night or to-morrow, and speak to Mr. Fuller. You can be thinking it over. You have been a good girl—I owe you something. If you can't stand it there—and I know you can't—I will give you papers of manumission and money to take you to Richmond. You have a close mouth—do not speak of this. Well, keep up heart and God bless you."

The master and servant parted—the one to ride wearily to his unpeaceful home, the other to journey along more hopefully to the shadeless cabins in the fields.

CHAPTER XIV

CHINA—UNCLE MAT'S PRAYER MEETING

Compared to the field-hands, who were little more than heathen and barbarian, our favorite China was a princess. One day and night among them proved to the unhappy girl that her master was in the right—she could not live with them. If she had met with suspicion, jealousy, and envy beneath her master's roof, she could not expect to escape it in her new home, where ignorance and all the baser passions ruled.

Toward night on the following day, which was Saturday, the master appeared at the cabins. He found China weeping disconsolately in the shade of a tree. So profoundly was she buried in her grief, she saw not her master until she heard his voice. For many hours had she watched his coming. When she had ceased to look for him, his kind voice aroused her to a momentary gladness.

"O, Master Duncan! Master Duncan!" was all she could utter.

"Bad enough, yes; I knew how it would be; I knew you would be willing to leave Kennons after you had tried this. I have just returned from Flat Rock; have had all the papers made for you; China, you are a free woman!"

"O, Master Duncan! good Master Duncan!" was all she could say again.

"Here, China, this is probably the last present I shall ever make you," handing to her a portmonnaie containing a few pieces of silver and gold, as also the invaluable papers of manumission. He withdrew it again as she was extending her hand, remarking:

"It is better, however, that it should be in the hands of Mr. Fuller. He is to go with you to-night to Flat Rock. You will remain at the 'Bald Eagle' until the train passes on Monday. You could remain at Petersburg if you chose, but my friends at Richmond can help you. I have written them, and they will see you properly cared for. Mr. Fuller will hand you this"—referring to the portmonnaie—"and you must guard it carefully. It is not sufficient that you carry it in your pocket; you should secrete it in some part of your dress, fastening it securely. You have a needle and thread? Well, then, do as I have told you. Be a good girl—honest and truthful; when I come to Richmond I will see you. There, don't cry now; you can yet be happy. I must have another talk with Fuller;"—seeing that personage approaching—"I shall not see you again; take care of yourself, and good-bye;"—and the master stretched down his hand—for he was still on horseback—which China grasped and presumed to kiss.

"There, that will do, my good girl; and don't forget what your Miss Ellice taught you."

This unusual reference to her former mistress was another stab for poor China. As her master rode away, she threw herself down upon the ground, making mournful moans that might have softened the hardest heart.

The field-hands, coming up from work an hour later, beheld with rage and dismay the intended victim of their malice mounted upon one of the fleetest horses upon the plantation, and Mr. Fuller all ready to mount another. He was but waiting to give additional orders to this unruly gang. This being done, each equestrian gave a slight stroke of the whip, and the horses galloped away from a hundred staring eyes.

"Let us fling a stone at her," said one.

"Let us set up a mighty howl," suggested a second.

"And git a mighty floggin' for yer pains," sneered a third, who was possessed of a grain of discretion.

China's heart lightened as she left the cabins and the intolerable red sands upon which they were situated. It was not the first time she had seen the uncouth faces and forms of the motley group who had been vengefully regarding her; but their appearance had seemed doubly appalling when viewed in the light of being her associates for life. Out of their sight she breathed freely again, and coming shortly into the main road, a feeling almost of joy seized her.

"I will not weep or be sad any more. I will leave the old life behind me, and Miss Rusha too, thank the Lord. Ah, poor Master Duncan! what a life he must live of it—the best master that ever servant had—good, kind Master Duncan! The trees hide Kennons from view; I shall not see it again. I would liked to have said farewell to Bessie, and to Chloe and Amy, and to Miss Rusha's Kizzie, too. I wonder if I ever shall see one of them any more;" and in spite of her resolution not to cry, China was obliged to wipe the tears that blinded her eyes.

Mr. Fuller was a model overseer. Nobody knew from what

quarter of the world he had hailed. He had been overseer for Duncan Lisle during seven years, and no one had ever heard him allude to any antecedents. He was a silent, reserved man of fifty years, perhaps, possessed good judgment, discerning sense of right and wrong, was inflexibly just, and invariably faithful to his word.

Duncan Lisle might well felicitate himself upon having secured so invaluable an assistant. He had never found, and was never expecting to find, his confidence misplaced. Trust begets trust, and master and overseer had become excellent friends.

Mr. Fuller had, however, a history of his own, but it lay away in England, where he prudently resolved to let it remain forever buried. For China he discharged his mission faithfully, exchanging with her only indispensable words, and, confiding to her care the precious portmonnaie, bade adieu both to her and to the "Bald Eagle," returning to Kennons after midnight.

China formed a pleasant acquaintance with the servants of the "Bald Eagle," and passed her Sunday very agreeably. At night she was invited to attend Uncle Mat's prayer-meeting. Uncle Mat was a personage of importance, not only in his own estimation, but in that of many others. His master was a drunken fellow, who had squandered most of his substance. By degrees he had lost the greater part of his plantation, had sold the most of his servants, his wife had died, children married and gone, and but for Mat he would have gone to utter ruin long ago. It was Mat who interfered in bloody quarrels, receiving blows and vituperations himself; it was Mat who walked by his master's side from elections, fairs, shows, etc., steadying him when he reeled, picking him up when he fell, dragging him from horses' feet and drunken men's knives, and keeping the breath of life in him by sheer watchfulness and unflagging exertion.

In return for this devotion, the master, Dick Rogers, gave but abuse of hand and tongue. But Uncle Mat was a Christian. He had a gift at prayer and exhortation. He could read, strange to say, and sing, of course. Mat was older than his master. Dick had been an only son, petted and spoiled. Mat had been his body-servant from his babyhood. Dick's father, upon his dying bed, had exacted from Mat a promise that he would always have a care for his reckless son. Mat had fulfilled his vow. Mat had learned to read by hearing the governess teach Dick. To shame the latter into diligence, it was a habit with Miss Train to call up the black boy, who exhibited more capacity and willingness than her pupil.

The servant was of a serious, reflective turn of mind. He became converted at a Methodist camp-meeting, and as he became a kind of preacher among his own people, he staid converted. He had one fault, to speak not of others. He was irascible to a great degree; a mosquito or a flea would drive him into a passion. But throughout his long career as guardian of his master, he had been never known to lose patience with him. Even mothers become vexed exceedingly with undutiful children; but this care of Mat for his worthless master exceeded even that of a mother for her child. Exceeded? Nay, we will say equalled.

It was somewhat rare in the slave States for servants to meet for religious purposes; insurrection might brood under such a cover. Mat, however, was so well known and so universally esteemed in his neighborhood, that he was allowed to hold his prayer-meetings every Sunday night.

It was to one of these that China went with her new-made friends. Nancy Carter's cabin was the meeting-house *pro tem*. It had been prepared for the occasion by an elaborate trimming of oak leaves and green boughs. Bouquets of flowers were interspersed with lights upon the preacher's stand. This invasion against white people's customs was due probably to the intense love which Afric's sons and daughters have for the "beautiful flowers."

Mat, tall and dignified always, seemed magnified in proportions and dignity when installed behind his stand of flowers and lights. His initial proceeding was invariably a great flourish of his white cotton handkerchief.

If Mat had a source of vanity deeper than another, it was of this above-mentioned article; and this, too, was so well known of him, that most of his presents consisted of handkerchiefs. He had, among his deposits, a good-sized box full of these useful and ornamental inventions. There was one from Lucy and Lizzie, four Sallies, three Dinahs, three Betties, two or three Janes, as many Anns, and hosts of others too numerous to mention. And every one of those donors looked steadily at the flourish of the preacher, if happily her own gift had come to the coveted honor.

The first prayer consisted of very large words very fervently uttered. This was comparatively brief, as a lengthy one for the whole world was to follow the first hymn.

Mat had adopted, of course, the custom of his superiors in the matter of singing. He read from the book the first two lines of the hymn, which the congregation seized and sung to the best of their ability. Two lines more were read, when music of voice, if not of words, became distinguishable.

Upon this occasion the preacher seemed troubled with unusual indistinctness of vision. He took his glasses from his nose more than once, violently rubbing them with his spotless handkerchief. Taking up his book for the third time, his eyes or his spectacles seemed still to be at fault. Perplexed and irritated, he exclaimed, unguardedly:

"Dog-gone-it! my eyes are dim; I cannot see to read this hymn."

The congregation supposing it all right, tuned up, and repeated it, though one would have been at great loss to make sense out of the myriad-syllabled confusion.

The preacher, surprised, attempted to explain. He said energetically, book still in hand:

"I did not mean to sing that hymn, I only meant my eyes were dim."

The simple people, still supposing the hymn to be continued, again poured forth volumes of sound.

In vain the preacher gesticulated, stamped, and threatened. So varied usually were the performances, this was thought to be but part of the programme. When the music hushed again the preacher cried:

"The devil must be in you all, that is no hymn to sing at all!"

Were those black people wilfully stupid? By no means. They did not know but they were doing as they had always done. The hymn-book was Greek to them, words were words; therefore they took up Uncle Mat's last words as innocently as if they had been

"On Jordan's stormy banks I stand,
And cast a wishful eye."

Uncle Mat's patience gave out completely; he hurled his

book at the musical leader's head:

"Dere, now see if ye can stop yer 'fernal noise. What bizness yer sing dat? Dats nothin' for to sing. You don't know nothin'. You biggest heap o' wooly heads I eber did see. Was der eber such a pack o' ignerant-ramuses eber in dis world afore? I answer 'firmatively—no! What's de use o' temptin' to preach to sich people? Dey wouldn't know if one was to rise from de dead. Not know de diff'rence 'tween psalm tunes an nuffin else! Dis people be dismissed."

The latter sentence was pronounced most disdainfully. The chorister, with head unbroken, and temper unruffled, arose and begged they might all be forgiven their heedlessness; it would be so great a disappointment to have the meeting broken up so prematurely, it would give them great pleasure if Uncle Mat would be *so* kind as to dispense with singing and proceed to prayers and exhortations. One or two other prominent members followed in much the same strain, flattering the indignant preacher by making special reference to his eloquence and popularity.

This had the desired effect. Uncle Mat became mollified, and wiping the angry perspiration from his brow, he embarked upon his longest prayer—during which our China and many others fell fast asleep.

CHAPTER XV

KIZZIE

"Lucy," said Mrs. Lisle, to a dwarfed child of thirteen years, who was one of those creatures expected to "run two ways at once," "run, Lucy, and tell Kizzie to come straight here to me."

The winged child came speedily back, accompanied by the weaver, a stolid looking old negress named Kizzie.

"Kizzie," exclaimed her mistress, "I know you have stolen the cover to that barrel that has been standing for so long outside the store-room."

"What for should I want wid de cover, Missis?" inquired the servant.

"That is for you to tell, and right soon too—do you hear me?"

"I have never touched the cover, Missis."

"I do not believe you. Who has then?"

"Sure, an' I doesn't know. You allus lays eberyting on to me,

Missis, when I'se jes as in'cent—"

"I wish to hear none of your palaver. You have stolen from me repeatedly; you know you have been just as hateful as you could be ever since—ever since Joe went away."

Mrs. Lisle had not designed this reference to Joe. Any mention of his name only made Kizzie more intractable.

Kizzie had been standing upon the threshold of her mistress' chamber, upon which she now sank down as if she had been shot. She had rolled herself into a ball, her grey head buried in her lap, from which issued the most protracted unearthly howl. This was succeeded by passionate ejaculations, in which "my poor Joe—my poor dear Joe, my baby—my last and only one"—were alone distinguishable.

"Kizzie, stop that acting, and get up from there," commanded Mrs. Lisle.

The ball swayed to and fro, but evinced no disposition for unbending.

"Bring me the whip, Lucy—we shall see."

The blows fell heavy and fast, but as for outward demonstration, cry or moan, that human form might as well have been a cotton bale.

The wearied hand of the mistress dropped by her side. She leaned against the casement panting for breath. Then Kizzie uprose tearless and stern.

"Miss Rusha, after this cruel floggin', I've a right to speak; but if you had a human heart I would not have this much to say. One after another ye sold my four big boys to the slave-buyer. You promised you would leave me my baby—my Joe. When he was fourteen years old you sold him too. You rob me of my five boys, and you 'cuse *me* of stealin' a barrel-cover! Miss Rusha, de judgments of de Lord will come upon you. Dis is my prayer, ebery day, ebery hour. Ye may whip, ye may kill—my prayer is mine own prayer to pray."

"Lucy," exclaimed Mrs. Lisle, now able again to speak, "run down to Thornton Hall and tell Mr. Hill to come here at once."

Mr. Hill was Mrs. Lisle's overseer.

"You will do no such thing, Lucy; and, madam, you have done enough," said the indignant voice of Mr. Lisle, who had entered upon the scene. "Go to your cabin, Kizzie; call for Amy and take her along with you."

Kizzie disappeared, and Mr. Lisle, meeting boldly the angered face of his wife, inquired into the origin of this disgraceful scene.

"Kizzie is mine, not yours. I have a right to do with my slaves as pleases me," said the wife.

"If you have a slave who deserves kindness at your hands, it is Kizzie. You have cruelly wronged her. To have killed her outright would have been a kindness compared to the injury you have inflicted upon her."

"How you talk, Duncan Lisle! One would think you a northern abolitionist. I understand whence you imbibed such principles"—sneeringly—"just as though one has not a perfect right to sell a slave if he wishes to! Don't talk to me in any such way. I have done nothing that I need be sorry for. But Kizzie is indeed the most hateful slave on the plantation.

I believe she steals just for the sake of stealing. What earthly use could she have for that cover, which she denies having taken, but which has mysteriously disappeared just when I happened to want it?"

"To what cover do you refer?" questioned her husband.

He was informed.

"I saw some little black fellows rolling something of the kind back of the stables this morning. Lucy, go hunt them up, and have the cover found. Is such a trifle sufficient to drive you into a passion, in which you accuse and punish an innocent person wrongfully?"

"I repeat to you, Mr. Lisle, that I shall do as I please with my own servants, and yours too, as you will find, and *have* found, I should think. Moreover, I am not going to be lectured by you as if I were a child"—Mrs. Lisle flung herself out of the room, to vent her bad humor upon whatever ill-starred persons should cross her path.

To do justice to Mrs. Lisle, she had intended to have sold both Kizzie and her son to the same buyer. As she herself said, she was always having trouble with Kizzie. There were times when she was positively afraid of her. Just before the proposed sale she had had a serious difficulty with her. Mistress and servant regarded each other as two enraged tigers might do, whenever they met. Mrs. Lisle made up her mind she would have Kizzie taken to the Court House and sold. Court was to be holden in a week or so; at such a time more or less slaves were put up at auction.

Kizzie was not sorry when informed of the proposed plan; though she shared, with others of her class, a horror of being "sold South," she had come to think she could not possibly fall into more cruel hands. Besides, in that region so terrible to the imagination of the slaves, she might come across one or all of her lost sons! At any rate, she would be beneath the same sky, and the dear hope of meeting them would be a continual comfort.

A whole day was consumed by Tippy—her real name was Xantippe—in plucking out Aunt Kizzie's grey hairs, and in fixing her up to appear to the best advantage for youth and sprightliness. She was only sixty, but hard labor and severe usage had told upon her heavily.

Aunt Kizzie, in her new linsey-woolsey and shining bandana as a turban, started off in great glee for the Court House. That she might appear there fresh, brisk, and pert, she was not suffered to walk, but Washington, the coachman, was ordered to drive her in the ark of the plantation wagon. Joe, smart, smiling, and newly-equipped in clothes, sat by her side, scarcely knowing whether he had best share in his mother's uncommon gaiety, or yield to his own anxious misgiving.

Another thing contributed to Aunt Kizzie's happiness. All the way to the Court House she was at perfect liberty to caress her nosegay of pinks and camomile. Kizzie had two grand passions; one was for her children, the other for her fragrant pinks. If she was allowed a garden patch the size of a hat-crown, it was devoted to her favorite flowers. She was wont to have her loom festooned with them; she drank in their perfume as did her web its woof; by night she had them scattered over her pillow, that, even in sleep, she might not lose their presence.

"I should think pinks would grow out of her nose," the servants were in the habit of remarking. It really often looked like they did, for, morning and evening, at her milking, her nose, instead of her hand, served as bouquet-holder.

Over the rough roads then, from Thornton Hall to the Court House, her attention was devoted to Joe and her pinks. She was to be sold—that was true—but then she had left a hated mistress. She had with her all she loved, her immense nosegay, her baby Joe, and, in her small bundle, her one pair of ruffled pillow-slips. She was starting out in the world again, and the world looked to her unaccountably new and beautiful.

It was morning now that shone upon Aunt Kizzie and her child. But night came, utterly dark and cheerless night, to both mother and boy. The two were put upon the block together. The boy showed for himself. But the sexagenarian human chattel was mercilessly scrutinized. She was made to sing, dance, and run. Her red turban was torn off, and in spite of the hirsutian manipulations to which she had been subjected, her wool appeared, like Shakspeare's spirits, mixed, black, white, and grey.

She was seized by the nose and chin, as if she had been a horse, and made to distend her jaws even painfully. She experienced a qualm or two when she thought of what a story her few remaining broken teeth would tell. Still, like the world and all the "rest of mankind," she had never fully realized that she had passed her prime and her usefulness.

This purchaser did not want her, nor did that, nor alas! the other! Each and every one were eager for the boy. The auctioneer's instructions had been to sell the two together, if possible, if not, at all events to sell the boy, as he would command a good price, and *money must be* raised.

Kizzie went wild when she saw her boy knocked off to a man who refused to take her, even as a gift!

O angels in heaven, what pitiful sights do ye not behold upon this earth of ours! Had ye no drop of balm from your vials of tender mercy to pour into the desolate heart of the stricken slave-mother, as she returned homeward in the dark, clutching frantically at her withered pinks, as did the talons of the vulture of grief at her wounded heart!

This blow to poor Kizzie occurred about the time of her mistress' marriage. The price of her agony, the money obtained for Joe, was sent to New York, and returned to Mrs. Rush in glittering jewels. Had this haughty woman been capable of realizing her sin, the showy baubles would have melted in the fiery furnace of her shame and contrition.

Kizzie became a changed woman; crazed, as some thought. Joe had been her baby, and her baby still at fourteen. How could her baby get along without his mother? This was the burden of her complaint, her unceasing utterance of sorrow. And still she lived on, sitting from morning until night at her loom, her tear of sorrow or sigh of despair inwoven with every thread, and from her bleeding heart going up the incessant prayer for Heaven's vengeance upon her persecutor.

One day, not far off, shall it not be more tolerable for Kizzie than for the beautiful mistress of Thornton Hall?

CHAPTER XVI

TIME AND CHANGE

Time and change! Why add the latter word? Doth not the former include all? Doth not time sadly overcome all things?

And this Time, which, according to Sir Thomas Brown, sitteth on a sphinx, and looketh into Memphis and old Thebes, which reclineth on a pyramid, gloriously triumphing, making puzzles of Titanian erections, and turning old glories into dreams—or something to that effect. This old Father Time, so much abused, misused, has given ten years to Kennons, ten years to Philip and his second wife in the far away homes of the Mussulman, ten years to the little Althea, who has bloomed into a beautiful girl of fourteen, beneath the roof of her loving guardians, John and Juliet Temple.

Ten years! and the fiery war of words has been followed by the deadlier fire of arms; civil war has raged over the sunny South, destroyed loving homes, mutilated fair forms, blotted out countless lives, and sent multitudes of souls unshriven before their Maker; but thanks be to God, riveted bonds have been broken and the slave hath been set free! Grand as was the sacrifice, infinite was the gain.

"I thought," said Amy, when she stood on her mount of

Pisgah, rolling up her melancholy eyes to the heaven, whence her deliverance had come, "I thought it would come some time, to our children, or our children's children, but not in my time, and to me! Moses was in de wilderness forty years; for what should I tink dat de Lord would gib us our liberty sooner'n to his own faithful servant? And we to have our'n in four years! But I knew it would come some time, sure as was a God in heaven. Hadn't we been prayin' and prayin', an' beseechin', an' how could de Lord stan' de prayers of such 'pressed, trodden people as we? Bress de Lord, O my soul, an' all dat is in me!"

Thousands like Amy sang their songs of deliverance. And like her, they arose from the sad waters of their Babylon, took their harps from the willows, seeking out joyfully new ways to lands of promise.

Those persons who had been kind, nay, even moderately just to their servants, were not at once abandoned. Some for months, some for years, were still faithfully served for hire. As a rule, however, the freed people scattered; but they went not far from their life-long homes. An innate love for early scenes and associations kept them where they might occasionally visit familiar persons and places.

Duncan Lisle was now a grave man of fifty. Threads of silver shone in his dark hair, but his tall form was erect and graceful as ever. He had become, in manner and speech, exceedingly reserved; his countenance wore almost habitually a melancholy, thoughtful expression. There were times, however, when his still attractive face lighted up with the old smile; and that smile revealed a gentle, noble spirit, still retaining its freshness unchafed by the carking cares and vexatious trials to which he had been daily subject. While to some men association with so peculiar and trying a nature as Rusha Thornton's might have brought moroseness and all unloveliness, Duncan Lisle, like the philosopher of hemlock fame, had turned his wife's shrewishness into a coat of armor, within which he preserved his soul serene, contemplative, and peaceful. This is saying very much for Duncan Lisle.

During the stormy period to which we have just referred, when the nation was in her throes of anguish, Mr. Lisle remained loyal to the Government. Aside from reason, common-sense, and humanity, he had seen more than enough in his wife's treatment of servants to disgust him with slavery. Though he took no active part, and, except when occasion required, preserved his usual reticence upon this subject also, he was nevertheless heart and soul upon the one side.

It is needless to observe that his wife was upon the other extreme. The idea of slavery was grateful to her intolerant nature. For herself she acknowledged no superior. The very God Almighty of Heaven she never took into *her* account. Had she been Lucifer among the angels, she too would have rebelled. Had she been daughter of Servius Tullius, she would have ridden over the dead body of her father. The golden rule was for others to practice, not for her; its Divine Author, the God-Man, was beyond her comprehension; His teachings fit but for underlings and slaves. Though scorning and hating the slave, she clung to slavery as if it were her life's blood. She poured forth all the venom of her nature upon the Northern foe, which was aiming to seize this petted horror from her grasp. She recalled often the tyrant's wish; like him would have given worlds had the subjects of Yankeedom but a single neck, that she might sever the Gorgonian head at one happy stroke.

She went almost wild upon the subject, and was the more violent that she could not draw her husband into her views. It was not enough that he should listen with apparent patience to her harangues, she demanded his verbal assent to her opinions. His silence, his attempts at evasion, provoked her equally as his firmly expressed disapproval. Nothing could satisfy her.

The marching of soldiers came even upon the grounds of Kennons. At times the noise and smoke of battle filled the atmosphere, as had the direful cholera thirty years before.

Rusha Lisle would have turned Kennons into an hospital for Southern soldiers. Even when her husband, hiding for his life, was hunted and dogged by rebel soldiers, her hand fed them with food; *her* hand that was never known to be stretched forth in charity to the deserving; nay, the roof, forbidden by prowling rebels to shelter its master, was proffered to his enemies by its dishonored mistress.

When tried beyond reason, Duncan Lisle arose in his wrath and asserted his mastery. Well might any true woman have quailed before that uprising, but not Rusha Thornton Lisle. A woman weaker-minded would have packed her silver, gathered her valuables, and fled to Thornton Hall, where she might harbor her dear rebels *ad infinitum*. This strong-minded woman well knew that by such a course of action she would be pleasing everybody but herself. She was not so fond of conferring happiness, nor so capable of self-sacrifice. So she continued to wage war within her household, more constantly vexatious to her husband, more tyrannous to her servants.

What added to Mrs. Lisle's bitterness was the conduct of her son. At the opening of hostilities, he had joined a rebel company, inflated with the idea that in a few weeks, or months at farthest, the Northern "mudsills" would be over-whelmed and out of sight. No one, except his mother, had talked louder and faster than himself. With his single hand he could slay a dozen of the cowardly Yankees.

After all this bravado, at the first smell of gunpowder, Thornton Rush threw down his firearms in a panic and ran as if from a sweeping tempest of fire and brimstone. Sleeping by day in hollow logs, traveling by night with haste and stealth, he made his way to the hated Northern lines, went as fast as cars could carry him to New York city, and, on a flying steamer, sneaked to Europe. There, once landed, he wrote his mother a letter. She had thought him dead, and mourned him proudly, as for a hero fallen for his country. She half read his letter, and threw it into the fire. Not dead, but a poltroon, a coward! She stamped her foot with contempt. *Her* son to lack courage?—*her* son a deserter from his post? She, woman as she was, would have gone into battle with the courage of a Caesar, the constancy of a Hannibal; but this son of hers, in whose veins flowed the cowardly northern blood, what could she expect of him, the son of Jude Rush?—and she curled her lip with contempt for both father and son. She ceased to mention his name, and revealed to no one that he still lived. Moreover, she disdained answering his letter, even had she not destroyed his written, but unread address and fictitious name.

Hubert Lisle, too, had volunteered, but it was to his country, and he was contending bravely, steadfastly, in the Northern ranks. Only good reports came back to Kennons of Ellice's brave son. This was galling to Rusha's pride; but it refuted silently her assertion that courage flowed not in Northern blood, for Hubert's mother had been a Northerner.

This young man, at the firing of Sumter, had passed his twenty-first year. He had graduated with honor from school and college, and was on the eve of embarking for Paris, where he was to pursue his medical studies. The call of his country stayed his uplifted foot, and placed in his not unwilling hand weapons of metal other than implements of dissection.

For three years Hubert was on active duty, when he became one of the unlucky prisoners at Salisbury. At the end of three months he was amongst the exchanged, and emerged from that infamous place such a walking skeleton as might have scared a ghost. Being unable to reenter the service, after several weeks recruiting in the hospital, he was permitted to visit Kennons.

That was a harder place for him than Salisbury. If it were not so trite, we would say he had fallen from Scylla upon Charybdis; or, if it were not vulgar, we might assert him to have fallen from the frying-pan into the fire; we will simply say, that not finding his father's wife at all agreeable, and having a remote suspicion that she might be tempted to put something that was not pure Java into his coffee, he left, after a few days, for the more congenial city where his college days had been spent.

The civil war, then, had come to a close. Men had fought bravely on either side. It is idle to assert that all the courage and gallantry was with one or with the other. Both Northerner and Southerner fought like men. Right conquered, and the South yielded gracefully enough. The humiliation of her proud spirit was sufficient for her to bear; taunts and sneers should have been spared her.

Mr. Fuller was still overseer at Kennons, and had managed with Mr. Lisle to retain a majority of the field-hands at a fair salary.

Of the house-servants, Amy and Chloe, being well advanced in years, offered to remain for the sake of their master. He, knowing what it must have cost them to make this resolve, and touched by their devotion, counselled them to leave at least the house. On the farthest corner of his plantation he would give them a few acres, build them a cabin, where, with their youngest children, they could live comfortably. This proposal they received with joy; they would be near the dear master, while removed from the authority of the mistress.

As to Rusha's servants, at the first announcement of freedom, every one went out from her presence forever, so soon as they could gather their wretched wardrobes into shape for departure. The most of them wore their all away, and that was sufficiently scanty. All went, we say. No, Kizzie remained. She was now a poor old woman of seventy. While watching the others depart, she sat down upon a rickety bench, folded her bony fingers over her knees, and cried silently. She was thinking. It would be hard either way, to go out among strangers, or to stay where her life had been so sorry and hopeless. She believed, on the whole, she would stay.

She did not like to leave her little cabin, where she had suffered so much, and where, after all, she had had her crumbs of comfort. How could she sleep out of her own bed, whose pillows were now ever adorned with her own article of luxury—ruffled pillow-slips? How could she leave that household god which stood day and night by her bedside, the cradle that had rocked her children? Should she find elsewhere a patch of ground for her darling pinks?

Besides, had there not been deep in her heart a hope that some time one of her boys—Joe, perhaps—might be led to seek his mother? How should he find her if she went out none knowing whither? Yes, she would stay.

Miss Rusha was glad of her resolution. She had hired a stranger for cook, and Kizzie, though now somewhat decrepit, could do her many a service. But it was not in this woman's nature to acknowledge a kindness; she acted and spoke as if she were doing this old servant a great favor by allowing her to remain.

It was but a few days ere Mrs. Lisle, who was now more than ever hasty in temper, raised her hand against Kizzie. Kizzie's eyes flashed, and she answered her mistress with angry words. This was more than Mrs. Lisle could bear, and she struck her a blow.

"A free woman to be whipped like a slave," thought Kizzie; "that time has gone by;" and she threatened to leave.

"Go whenever you please," said the lady.

But Kizzie could not go, and did not. She had borne so much, she might endure a little more.

Her pertinacity in staying induced Mrs. Lisle to throw off all restraint. She believed nothing would force her to leave, and fell back to her former mode of treatment of this pitiable woman. There came a limit, however, to Kizzie's endurance. She packed up her few goods, firmly resolved to see her mistress' face no more. She would stay a few days at Amy's and Chloe's, and then go farther. She would have taken up her abode altogether with them, as Mr. Lisle advised, only that she and those amiable women had not been the best of friends. Kizzie had been too solitary and brooding to form a pleasant companion. At the last moment she might again have hesitated had she not already sent her parcels ahead of her by a chance black man.

Having cast a last lingering look about her cabin, she leaned over her cradle, which she wet with her tears. Then going into the sunlight, she bent down over her patch of pinks, which were now in fullest fragrance. She had fallen on her knees, bowing over, and burying her wrinkled face in the rich mass of bloom and beauty.

Kizzie's heart had not broken over the cradle, nor was it doomed to break over her beloved blossoms. A man's step startled her. Raising her head, a tall, dignified military officer of color met her view. He approached her close, looking steadily at her with those smiling, pleasant eyes which Kizzie had never forgotten, could never forget, were they in her Joe of fourteen, or in this fine looking officer. Her heart said—"It is my Joe; my baby Joe," but her lips could not syllable a word.

"Mother," said the trembling, glad voice, though so deep and heavy, "you still love your pinks, mother, do you still love your Joe?"

Ah, what a meeting was that! The wonder is that Kizzie survived it. Sorrow, grief, had not killed, neither did joy.

When Joe told his mother he had come for her to accompany him North, she proposed taking her pinks, earth and all.

"O no mother, I have a house and garden of my own; you shall have a place for your pinks as large as you wish."

The old woman looked up at him questioningly. Before she could speak he said:

"I see what you wish to know, yes, I am married." "And have a baby Joe" too, he would have added, only that he had resolved his mother should be taken by surprise in the visible knowledge of her grandchild.

It was not now difficult for Kizzie to leave her old home; and as she journeyed northward astonished by new scenes, she learned from Joe his history since their painful separation.

He had grieved so for his mother that his new master thought it best to part with him in a neighboring State. He had fallen into good hands; he had learned to read and write. At the breaking out of the war he had deserted his master and escaped North. Here he had enlisted as a soldier, and after much active service had been raised to rank of Lieutenant in his company. He had found time to marry a runaway slave-girl, whom he sent North. He and she were both prudent and industrious, and when the war was over had means to purchase them a comfortable home. He had always been determined to revisit his mother. The visit had been doubly pleasant, since he had fought for her liberty and his own.

When Kizzie arrived at her son's home, and was introduced to his wife and the unsuspected baby, she was again speechless. But her silent prayer was that her years might be lengthened out to the number of Methuseleh's, in order long to enjoy this unaccustomed happiness.

CHAPTER XVII

THE ST. LEGERS

John Temple had been a three month's volunteer at the commencement of the war. But his business so much suffered, and his absence so distracted his wife, that he considered it his duty, after his term of service had expired, to remain at home. John Temple, for the son of an Irishman, was a man of a great deal of equanimity. He could face a body of soldiers without flinching, and he could meet daily the frivolousness and folly, the bagatelles and boutades of his pretty wife without losing patience. That he could do the one was not strange or uncommon; but to do the other without seeking the satisfaction of slamming a door, kicking a footstool across the floor, or boxing the children's ears, was truly remarkable.

It was well for Juliet that she had married a man whose disposition and temperament was so the reverse of her own. She was one of those who delight in fancying her own life to be filled with more trials and troubles than any other person's can be. And why? She had a beautiful home, rich and fashionable in its appointments, plenty of servants at her command, horses, carriage and driver at her disposal, a niece of remarkable loveliness and beauty, a son and daughter somewhat spoiled, who inherited fortunately their mother's beauty and their father's good sense; a kind and indulgent husband—what more could she wish?

Ah, Juliet Temple! the hand of sorrow had never touched thee. The sacred form of grief had passed thee by. Death had flitted around thee, taking others, leaving thee and thine. Father and mother, brother and sisters, husband and children all remained to thee! Yet did'st thou never raise thy heart in thanksgiving unto God, but suffered it to be depressed and fretted at the nameless trifles that came vexingly.

Few persons, like Juliet, live to the age of thirty-five without having suffered losses and afflictions. Juliet never paused to consider this. She never reflected, even at a funeral, that thus far she had been spared, but that her turn must come. When she gazed upon poverty and distress no thought that such might have been, or might still be hers, crossed her mind. She was more unhappy than the cripple or the beggar that passed her by.

To such souls come awakenings, soon or late; sometimes gentle, sometimes startling as an earthquake.

Captain St. Leger, who had seldom visited home of late years, on a recent return had taken with him his invalid wife to China. He had opened business relations at a principal port, which had gradually become his more usual stopping place and home. Mrs. St. Leger had improved somewhat on the voyage; and the first letter received from her on her arrival was favorable. Little then were the daughters prepared for the succeeding letter which contained intelligence of her death.

The long illness of their mother had prepared the elder daughters in a measure for the event. Juliet had not anticipated such a thing. She had thought only of seeing her mother return from her lengthy voyage recruited in health and spirits, with her old taste and ability revived for society and amusements. She shut herself up in a room and grieved inordinately. Had her own and father's household lay dead before her, she could not have assumed a wilder sorrow. In vain her husband soothed and reasoned. Her mother had been a great sufferer; she could not expect but that she must some time die; she was beyond the reach of pain; for her the agony of death was over. All to no purpose. She would have no comfort in husband, children, or sisters; her mother was dead, and she would not be comforted.

John Temple thought it would do her good to see Dr. Browne; he accordingly sent for him, and without her knowledge.

Dr. Browne called; but to see him Juliet persistently refused. The real reason was because she was in wretched *deshabille*, her face was swollen with weeping, and it would be such a weary work to do her hair. No; her vanity was yet stronger than her grief, and she would not be seen by Dr. Browne.

Two months passed, and Juliet had recovered her usual composure, if composure can be used in connection with so unrestful a creature.

And now came a letter from the hand of a stranger, bearing news of the sudden death by apoplexy of Captain St. Leger.

This was indeed unexpected, and created in the family a much greater sensation than had the death of the mother.

The Van Rensaleers and the Langs began to inquire about the condition of the property. Without consulting Mr. Temple, the husbands of Leonora and Estelle sailed at once for China.

Juliet's anxiety about her share of the estate somewhat modified her grief in this instance. She had but slightly known her father; he had been home but seldom, and for brief visits. He was an austere man, very fine-looking, but silent and undemonstrative. She should not miss him so much, still his death was such a shock—as she was fond of repeating to her friends; she should never recover from the effects of two such terrific shocks.

So selfish in her grief was Juliet, nobody's sorrow had ever been like unto her own. Whereas, had she only stopped to consider, had she been a Christian instead of a heathen, a woman instead of a child, she would have borne silently this affliction as a necessary dispensation of Providence; she would have bowed her heart humbly before God, kissing the hand that had chastened her, thankful that those nearer and dearer had been left unto her.

The two elder brothers-in-law in due time returned from their mission with the doleful intelligence that the late Captain St. Leger had died insolvent, so far as his foreign wealth was concerned. They swore in open court, for Mr. Temple summoned them to appear and obliged them to take oath, that they received not sufficient from the assets to defray the expenses of their voyage.

Of this Juliet was disposed to believe not a word. Her brothers-in-law had ever been ill-disposed toward her because she married for love, and looked down on Temple because he had industriously labored for his wealth instead of having received it, like themselves, from dishonest or thrifty grandfathers. She believed they had connived together to enrich themselves at her expense.

Here, then, was another ground for anxiety. She begged Mr. Temple to institute legal proceedings, and have the matter thoroughly sifted. Mr. Temple liked no man to believe he was to be tamely cheated, and was at first disposed to accede to Juliet's suggestion. Upon farther reflection, however, he thought it wiser to let the matter drop. Aside from anxiety, the expenses would be great. His adversaries had taken time by the forelock, and had taken care doubtless to cover up their tracks.

He was now independent; his business needed all his attention; he would not risk the certain for the uncertain. He would look out for his share yet unappropriated in the city, though Captain St. Leger, at his last visit home, had given deed to Juliet of the house she since her marriage had occupied.

But the settlement of the St. Leger estate does not materially concern us. It had the effect, however, of completely alienating Juliet from her sisters.

Leonora was still childless, though she had so far changed her resolution as to have received two children into her house. She could scarcely have done otherwise. It had been announced by letter from Philip that a cargo of eleven children from his mission were about to sail, and would reach New York at about a given time. Three of these children were his, and he hoped his sisters would find places for them in their families, and interest themselves in seeking good homes for the remaining others.

Philip wrote that expediency alone could have induced them to part with the dear children. Their hearts were torn asunder, etc., etc. The touching letter was read from the preacher's desk. There was not a dry eye in the house, nor a heart that did not long to clasp the foreign missionary waifs. The trouble was not in getting homes in sufficient number for the children—there were not enough children for the homes offered. It would be such a blessed privilege to have a missionary's child in the house. The various Judson children that were scattered here and there were perpetual curiosities. Their very presence was enough to sanctify, dignify, and make illustrious any house wherein they might dwell.

There never occurred to Philip when he wrote, to the city preacher when he read, nor to the congregation who listened to the pathetic story of the "hearts torn asunder," an idea as to the incompatibility of missionary life with raising a family of children; nor that each and every missionary father had better have given his heart a decided wrench in the beginning, by abstaining from marriage, than have been a victim to perpetual domestic anxiety and have suffered such ever-recurring wounds.

At first Leonora had taken Philip's three children, although a childless, wealthy couple had offered to adopt the eldest, a boy of nine years. He was handsomer and finer looking than his two little sisters, who were both quiet and pretty. Leonora thought she should have something to be proud of in the boy, who was a St. Leger thoroughly, and might readily enough be mistaken as her own son.

She was not long, however, in discovering that she had taken more upon herself than she could bear. This handsome nephew was the exact counterpart of what his father had been at similar early age. Leonora remembered well that Philip had been an imp of mischief, and that she had suffered torments on his account. This young Marius—named for Mary Selby in full—like his father before him, seemed to think his young sisters made for no earthly purpose but for his amusement. If they were out of his presence he was wretched; when with them he left them no peace; he would fling at them paper darts, almost strangle them with an impromptu lasso, demolish their playhouse, decapitate their dolls, and do all the mischief his really inventive genius could suggest.

Leonora knew how worse than vain would be all reasoning with such a subject. The example of her brother was all she needed. She took him in her carriage, and set him down, with his baggage, at the door of the wealthy couple who had been so anxious to gain possession of him. She was not surprised, two weeks later, to learn that he had been transferred to the family of the Presbyterian clergyman, nor shortly after to be informed that a collection had been taken up among the wealthy members of the church for his education at a country school; to this she was invited to contribute, which she did liberally.

Captain St. Leger had given all his city property to his daughters, leaving his only son unprovided for.

As to Estelle, Mrs. Lang, she rejoices in five daughters, which, added to her four sons, makes her family equal in number, if not in degree, to that of Queen Victoria's. She has had a wing added to her already extensive mansion, wherein she has had her children installed, with their nurses at command, one being an aged lady, trusty and faithful. Unlike Juliet, Estelle became wise enough to give over fretting and borrowing trouble. She goes much into society, though less devoted to it than her elder sister, but looks considerably to her household affairs, and on the whole makes a tolerable wife and mother. She would be religious perhaps if she knew how to be. But this she has never learned at St. Mark's Church, and she knows not where else to go.

CHAPTER XVIII

ST. MARK'S OR ST. PATRICK'S?

A few months later, and Juliet Temple, with her niece and children, returned from St. Mark's, whither they had been for morning service.

"I declare this is the last time I shall go out to church while this hot weather continues," exclaimed Juliet, throwing herself upon the parlor lounge, not having sufficient strength to mount the stairs. "I was a dunce for going to-day," she continued, having panted awhile for breath, and fanning herself with a feather fan; "there were but few out; almost none at all of the fashionables. Let me see: there was Dr. Elfelt's pew vacant, the Shreves' vacant, the Dunns', and the Quackenboss'; not one of the Herricks, Messengers, nor Livingstons there; you'll not catch me there again with only such a common crowd; it is high time Dr. Browne shut up for the summer, though somebody said he wasn't going to shut up this summer, there has been such a hue and cry in the papers about this shutting up of churches; but he might as well, I can warn him, or he will preach to empty pews; it beats all, and to-day was communion day, too; I should have thought more would have turned out; but, I declare, I thought I should smother when I went up to the rails; and, to cap all, that old Mrs. Godfrey, who weighs at least three hundred, came and knelt close by me, and just completely crushed all one side of my flounces; I was provoked and indignant; this, added to the intense heat, was almost insupportable; but here I am again, thank God. O, Althea, you look so cool and comfortable; won't you come, please, and fan me a minute—untie my hat, and take away my gloves and scarf, they are like so many fire-coals. It is too bad to make a servant of you, dear, but that is just the way, the girls stay so long at their Mass, as they call it; I wouldn't have Catholic girls just for this very reason, that they insist always upon going to Mass, only that I really can trust a good Catholic girl better than anyone else. If a girl calls herself Catholic, but is not particular about her religious duties, I am on the watch for her; but a girl that insists upon going through thick and thin, heat and cold, such a girl I trust in spite of me. Now, Johnny, bring me a glass of ice-water, dear. And daughter, if you will just step up to my room and bring my salts, you will be a darling. Dear me! shall I ever get cool again? If you will just bring me that sofa pillow, but no, it will be too hot. I wish I had a nice pillow from my own bed, the linen slips would be so refreshing."

Althea started to go for one, when her aunt pleased again to change her mind.

"On the whole, I think now I will be able to go up stairs, and you can unlace my tight boots, they are just killing my poor feet, and I can get into my wrapper; yes, that will be nice."

And Juliet started briskly for her chamber. She met her daughter at the foot of the stairs with the tiny cut-glass bottle.

"You can bring it back; I have concluded to go up myself; and, Johnny, that is right, my son, bring the waiter up stairs, where, if I am not completely exhausted first, I will try to get comfortable."

The stream of Juliet's talk ceased not to flow, while her niece, son, and daughter flew hither and thither, as was dictated by her caprice.

At length, in her snowy wrapper, she half reclined gracefully upon an equally snowy lounge, which she had ordered drawn to the darkest corner of the room.

"Now, Johnny and Flora dear, you can go anywhere you please, until the girls come and lunch is served. Althea will stay and fan me, and perhaps I can sleep," said this selfish woman, languidly closing her eyes.

She had done talking enough for any one member of a sociable; and Althea, commendably preserving her patience, devoutly hoped the poppy-god, of which she had lately been reading in her Virgil, would shower well the eyelids of her Aunt. Vain hope! The uneasy tongue again commenced:

"I wonder how your uncle endures it! Every week-day at his counting house—every Sunday twice at Mass, and then again at Vespers. It is all of six months now since this very pious fit came over him. And strange to say, I believe I brought it about myself. I never had given up the notion of his coming around to be with me a High Churchman. He always *was* the most honest soul—the offer of thrones and kingdoms could never induce him to tell a lie—but as to what he called his religious duties, he had become very careless; I could easily coax him to stay from Mass when I did not feel like dressing for St. Mark's, but about six months ago, I think it was, I undertook to convert him to my way of thinking, and to make him see how vain and wicked these Romish practices were, when he astonished me by his earnest defence of them, and ever since he is a perfect enthusiast; wouldn't stay from Mass if the house was on fire, and if you would believe it, is actually insisting that the children shall go with him whenever they don't go with me; next thing will be to take them with him anyhow, and the idea of having Johnny and Flora brought up to believe that it is a mortal sin to be absent from Mass, even when the day is scalding hot, or piping cold! That is downright tyranny. I would never endure it! It is well I was never brought up a Catholic; they'd find a rebel in me, sure. All the priests, and Bishops, and the Pope, and a hundred like him, couldn't oblige me to go to church, if I was not a mind. And Althea, only think of it, your uncle, good as he is, every month now goes on his knees to Father Duffy and confesses his sins! That is too much. Your uncle, Althea, if I do say it, who am his wife, is the best man in the world—the very best, and the idea! Why, I believe it is the other way, and this priest, Mr. Duffy, had better go on *his* knees to my husband—he would have more to say, I'll wager. John Temple is sensible upon everything else, but upon the matter of his religion he has become childish and absurd. I believe he would give me up and the children too, dearly as he loves them, rather than his religion. There he is at last," she exclaimed eagerly, as the hall door opened below, and a man's foot was heard ascending the stairs.

"O John! I am so glad you have come. You have almost been the death of me though, you naughty man."

"How so, Juliet?"

"Why, did you not tell me when I objected to going to St. Mark's that if I did not go and take the children you should take them with you?"

"I did."

"Well, of course, rather than to have them go to that Irish Church, I made a martyr of myself and went with them to St.

Mark's, but it is for the last time this summer, I can promise you. Why, I have almost died with the heat."

"It is a very warm day, unusually warm for the season," was the only response.

"And is that *all*, John, that you have to say? You are *not* going to take the children hereafter to church with you, when it is impossible for me to go with them to St. Mark's?"

"That is what I told you, Juliet. I have thoroughly made up my mind, and—"

"O, don't tell me you have made up your mind," cried the lady hysterically, who knew from a twelve years' experience that John Temple's made-up mind was like an adamantine wall to all her feeble missiles.

"Juliet," he replied firmly, "I will no longer see our children growing up without religious training. And this very day I have formed a new resolution. Johnny and Flora are to go with me every morning to early Mass. This is a subject which must be no longer neglected;" and here Mr. Temple, having loosened his necktie, and donned dressing-gown and slippers, took up the fan that Althea had dropped upon his entrance, and seated himself by his wife.

Juliet, as usual, betook herself to tears. But tears did not always drown her tongue; certainly not upon this occasion.

"I don't see how it is possible for a man, generally so kind and good, to make himself so obstinate and disagreeable. You don't find me so obstinate; do I not often yield to you, John Temple, I would like to know?"

"You look upon but one side, Juliet; we are man and wife;

our religions are different. I speak not of yours, I know only my own, and this, my own religion, binds me to bring up my children in the fear and love of God. You may, for some reasons, be attached to your religious service, but the rules of your Church have no binding force upon you. For you it is no sin to allow your children to attend Mass. Your Church claims to be a branch of ours, admits ours to be the true Church of Christ, from which it sprang. In attending Mass with me, your children are still within the fold of the Church. With me it is different. I believe in but one Church. All others so-called, however well-intentioned, have not the banner of Christ, not unto them were given the promises of our Divine Lord. For me it is a mortal sin to allow my children any longer to remain in their present state. Johnny should have been already well instructed, and ready for First Communion and Confirmation."

"O, John! when you know I am so dreadfully opposed to it, how can you insist upon having the dear children brought up in such a way. It will ruin their prospects for life. Likely as not Johnny would become a cruel priest, and our sweet little Flora would be dragged into a convent."

"Don't be a fool, Juliet," said Mr. Temple, losing his patience, "who talks about dragging people into convents? Not Catholics. Have you not confidence in me, and will you not believe when I assure you I could not ask a higher, nobler place for our children than that you so deprecate? Thus far have I yielded to you in this matter. But, Juliet, who has made me father and master in this house? Unto God shall I have to render my account; and though I would spare your feelings, I must still be true to my conscience."

"As far as the religion itself goes, I don't care so much," responded Juliet, attempting to dry her eyes with her handkerchief, already saturated, "but what grieves me to the heart, what I cannot bear nor tolerate is this association with the low and vulgar," the one idea still uppermost in the weak woman's mind.

"Juliet, are you never to have thoughts higher than those that pertain to society and fashion? Do you never think the time is surely coming when you must give up all these things to which you are attached, when death must come to you, and a new life, and have you no care as to what that life shall be?"

The lady shivered and covered up her eyes.

"Why do you talk thus to me? Do you not know that I have a perfect horror of such things? O, John, the very thought of dying almost distracts me. *Must* we all die? How I wish we could live forever, and never grow old! When we get very old, John, then, if I should be taken sick, I want you to hold me strong by the hand that death may not take me."

"But, Juliet, if you should be taken sick before you are old?"

"I have no fear, John, while you are with me, even though I be sick. Do you not know, have you not learned, that I fear nothing when with you, and have a good hold of your hand? In a thunder-shower I am so timid without you, I think every bolt is to strike me; if you are near, but you must be close, I have no fear. It seems nothing can harm me if you are by. So, John, while I have you, I have no fear of death."

Mr. Temple had dropped the fan, and Juliet's two little hands were nestled in his strong, broad palms. He looked with tenderness into the face upturned so trustfully to his.

"But if I should die, Juliet, and you should not have me?"

Juliet gave a piercing scream and threw herself into her

husband's arms. Was it for the first time such a thought had ever been presented to her mind? Life without her husband! She could not conceive of it. It seemed as if he had always been with her; as though he had become so much a part of herself that she could not live without him. For, though she wearied and annoyed him, teased, opposed, and vexed him, she loved him beyond all things, even her children. Beneath all her vanity, folly, and thoughtlessness throbbed one passion deepest of all, love for her husband.

"My poor little wife," said John Temple, when he could again speak, "I am frail and human, but there is One mighty and eternal. I am weak and erring, but there is One strong and infallible. Put your trust in One worthier than I; lay your hand in His who shall lead you by the still waters of peace; in His which shall never fail you, neither in life, death, nor eternity."

CHAPTER XIX

"IN SUCH AN HOUR AS YE THINK NOT"

During the following week Juliet Temple was more serious than usual. She often found herself wondering why her husband had spoken to her in such mournful words. They haunted her the more she attempted to drive them away; she could not even reflect with indignation upon his avowed purpose as regarded the children. His solemn tones and manner had taken the sting from his unwelcome resolutions.

Once she referred to the subject:

"Your sermon of last Sunday has sunk deep in my heart. It is the only sermon that has ever done me any good—or harm," she added.

"I did not intend to trouble you; but you know I would like to see you more thoughtful."

Had John Temple taken this course long ago with his wife, she would have become perhaps a wiser, better woman. But he loved peace and quiet; and he probably thought also that no serious words from him could make impression upon her preoccupied, impervious mind.

John Temple was true to his word. For several mornings his children were kneeling by his side at Mass, ere their mother had awakened from her slumbers. He himself heard their daily lessons in Catechism.

When Saturday came around Juliet began to think about the children going to St. Patrick's next day. She was so surprised at herself for having acquiesced so readily. True, she knew it was no use to combat her husband upon the point, but she might not have appeared to him to yield so easily. Instead, however, of any disposition to disapprove, she began to think how it would be were she to go herself. Pshaw! Where was all her pride, that she should begin to think of going to church with her Jim, Bridget, and Ann? But somehow, for the first time, she did not like to think of her husband going without her. He had spoken so solemnly of the possibility of his some time leaving her! Hereafter she should feel as if he must not go out of her sight. She put away her embroidery for her crochet. In turn, her crochet was tedious, and dropping it, she took up a book which her husband had been reading at leisure moments the last day or two.

The book she had never before observed. It was "The Following of Christ." She opened where was his mark; and this mark was, for this time, a tiny rose she had handed him that very morning. She pressed to her lips the rose, which was yet fragrant, though faded. She commenced to sing carelessly:

"Ye may break, ye may ruin the vase if ye will,
But the scent of the roses will hang round it still,"

when the heading of the Chapter, which the rose had marked, caught her eye, "Of the thoughts of death."

"A very little while and all will be over with thee here. See to it, how it stands with thee in the next life. Man to-day is, and to-morrow he is seen no more. If thou art not prepared to-day, how wilt thou be to-morrow?

"To-morrow is an uncertain day, and how knowest thou if thou shalt have to-morrow?"

"No wonder his mind is sober and solemn, with such reading as this," mused Juliet, but she continued.

Fire bells commenced to ring. Was this so uncommon an occurrence as to cause Juliet to drop her book and press her hand to her heart?

"What does it mean? I am so fearfully nervous. It is not our house that is on fire."

She walked to a window; ah, the fire was near, but a few squares distant; the slight wind, however, would bear it in an opposite direction. There was no occasion for fear. Juliet took up her book again, and read a few pages. She was reading these passages a second time, and with something like a thrill of awe, for they seemed to be spoken to herself:

"Be therefore always in readiness, and so live that death may never find thee unprepared.

"Many die suddenly and unprovidedly; for the Son of Man will come at the hour when He is not looked for.

"When that last hour shall have come, then thou wilt begin to think far otherwise of all thy past life; and great will be thy grief that thou hast been so neglectful and remiss."

The door-bell rang violently. Juliet made an effort to rise from her chair, but sank back weak as an infant. Her face turned deadly pale, and she clenched the closed book in her pallid hands.

There was a confused sound in the room below; the tread of men and subdued voices. Suddenly, above these, she caught a groan. This broke the spell; she flew rather than walked to the small parlor so strangely occupied.

A knot of men separated slightly as she drew near. O God of Heaven, was that her husband? John Temple, who went out a few hours ago brave and strong, in the full vigor of beautiful manhood, blighted, disfigured, burned in the fiery furnace?

"My child, my child," had a frantic woman screamed as she was borne down a ladder in the powerful arms of a fireman.

"My child," she still cried from the ground, her eyes upraised to the window of flame, her hands clasped in pleading agony. Eager eyes looked upward, but even brave hearts hesitated to rush into the sea of flame.

It was madness, but John Temple ventured. They would have held him back, but in that supreme moment of supernatural exaltation of courage he was strong as well as bold. As he would others should do for him so would he do for them. It was the thought of his wife and children that nerved him to such heroic, desperate effort, and alas, so unavailing!

Streams of water had darkened the fiery mass, and hope began to whisper to the eager crowd.

Yes, John Temple stepped out upon the slippery, blackened ladder, grasping the inanimate form of a little child. Loud cheers rent the air. But they pierced the hearts of those who bent over the senseless forms of the deliverer and the child. Most of their clothing, their hair, and eyebrows were burned, they were fearfully scarred, and worse than all they had breathed the flames! Physicians were on the ground, prompt assistance was rendered, and John Temple again drew breath. With the child there was a moan, a gasp, and all was over.

This was the result of a kerosene explosion. So instant had been the ignition of everything combustible that nearly the whole interior was in flames before assistance could arrive. Stout engines played but upon useless debris, and saved only unsightly walls.

Some friend of John Temple had run for the priest, and by the time he was laid in his own house Father Duffy too had arrived. The sufferer had become sensible, but could not speak. He was evidently in fearful agony.

Three physicians looked at each other and shook their heads. They had the wife to care for now, who, with piercing shrieks, fell insensible at their feet.

"Will you leave me alone with him a moment," said the priest, and the others withdrew, bearing away the stricken woman.

It was but for a few moments indeed. The dying man could only make signals in answer to questions, and received the *Viaticum* with eyes raised in thankfulness. The physicians had not been able to get him to swallow, but this blessed bread of life, this comforter by the way, this solace and support through the dark valley, nature nor suffering did refuse. It was pitiful to see him attempt to fold in reverence his inflamed and swollen hands, and to make, as his last expiring effort, the beloved sign of our holy religion.

To John Temple death had come suddenly indeed, but not unprovidedly. He had been moved, no doubt by heavenly inspiration, to make a general confession only the Sunday previously. And Father Duffy had reason to believe it had been made with that care, diligence, and fullness as if he had known it to have been his last. We have seen what an impression had been made upon his mind in his interview with his wife.

Upon recovering consciousness, Juliet demanded to be admitted to her husband. Disguises and delays she would not brook, and they led her back. Her children were now there, and Althea, and further back the servants. These latter were upon their knees, with the priest, saying prayers for the dead.

Let us here draw a veil. We have been disgusted with Juliet, out of all patience with her levity and unwomanliness, but we sympathize in her unutterable grief. Hard must be the heart unmoved by those wildest moans, those saddest plaints.

"Do not weep," said Dr. Browne to her after the funeral, "it is vain, worse than vain."

"Only tears are left me," she half-uttered.

"Your children!"

"They only speak to me of him."

"But yourself; for your own sake do not thus yield to immoderate grief."

"I tell you, Dr. Browne, my heart shall dash itself against this sorrow till it break—break!" she exclaimed wildly.

"But this is not Christian submission."

"I am not a Christian, Dr. Browne; you cannot expect from

me submission. Do you expect grapes from thorns?"

"Not a Christian, Mrs. Temple?"

"You know I am not a Christian, Dr. Browne! I have never known but one Christian in my life, and that was John Temple."

Dr. Browne felt somewhat scandalized. A member of his church to say boldly she had never known but one Christian, and that Christian a Roman Catholic; was it not incomprehensible? But then Mrs. Temple was not now in her usual mind. Due allowance must be made, and he would seek a more favorable opportunity for renewing the subject. He arose to leave.

"What shall I do, Dr. Browne? I cannot bear day nor night; life is a torture; I cannot bear life, nor can I endure to think of death. O, help me, Dr. Browne."

"Only God can help you, Mrs. Temple, and I pray that His grace may be sufficient for you."

"But you forget that I have no God."

"Mrs. Temple, you are beside yourself. No God?"

"No! He is afar off, or I am shut out from Him. I have never known Him. I cannot pray to Him."

"When you shall be more collected I will call again. Meantime, you will find much comfort in our Book of Common Prayer. Have recourse to it and to the throne of grace."

Juliet abandoned herself as much to remorse as to grief.

She had had the best of husbands; she had been to him the worst of wives. As in a mirror, she saw all her past life. She remembered how fretful and fault-finding she had been; how difficult to please, how unlovely she had made herself. If John could come back, only just long enough for her to tell him how very, very sorry she was, how much she loved and respected him, how he had always done everything right, and she had been ever in the wrong; but he could not come even for that. She collected around her the various articles he had used; among others, his rosary, crucifix and prayer-book. How careful he had been to keep them hidden away, where they might not offend her eye, or provoke her ridicule and sneer. She read every day, in the "Following of Christ," the chapter John had last read, which the faded rose still marked.

In this was a kind of comfort, but there was peace nor rest in aught else. She walked the floor distractedly, and wrung her hands and tore her garments. She shut herself up in the darkness, and stretched forth her hands and prayed the spirit of John to come back to her in pity. She would not admit her sisters; her children she allowed to grieve alone.

Suddenly, came back to her the memory of a look of pity and compassion, which she had forgotten. When she had returned, on that memorable day, to her husband, who had just breathed his last, as she raised her eyes, scarcely daring to let them fall upon the dear face, she encountered the gaze of Father Duffy. He had, unconsciously, looked upon this bereaved woman, whom he knew to be without the fold, therefore, without suitable consolation for this trying moment, as our dear Lord may be supposed to have looked upon Mary and Martha, when they informed Him that Lazarus, their brother, was dead.

The remembrance of this compassionate look softened Juliet's heart toward the priest. For the first time in her life, she began to think he might be something beside an impersonation of evil. To John he had been a father and a friend; might not she have confidence in one he had so loved and trusted?

She began to wish he would call. She wondered he did not, if but to see after the children. He must be aware of John's recent action in regard to them, perhaps may have counselled the same. The more she thought of this, the stronger, by degrees, became her desire to see and consult him.

Juliet was what might be termed a "person of one idea." Not that her ideas never changed—she was very versatile; but she was animated wholly by one idea at a time, to the exclusion of all others. Two weeks ago, the Catholic Irish priest was the last person she would have thought of with desire to see. Now, of all people in the world, it was from Father Duffy she would seek counsel.

She rang her bell, and when Ann appeared, thus addressed her:

"You may do my hair, Ann; I have changed my mind; I thought I would never have it touched again by comb or brush, but I will. You need not be particular; only get the tangles out and let it hang; you can find a black ribbon somewhere. I don't care any more how I look, besides, I am only going to see your priest, Mr. Duffy. He must be used to seeing people in all sorts of rigs. It would be different if I were to meet Dr. Browne. I would dress for him as for a king, once; but not now! I never shall care again how I look; poor John cannot see me."

Sobs and tears choked further utterance. Ann gave a quick start, when her mistress mentioned the priest's name. She could hardly believe she had heard aright. She was used to almost every caprice from Mrs. Temple, but this last transcended every other. What did it portend?

Mrs. Lang, who was about the size and height of Mrs. Temple, had kindly taken upon herself the care of procuring her sister's mourning. Having submitted to all the troubles and inconveniences, she had, but the day before, sent home several dresses. She would herself have accompanied them, had she not repeatedly been refused admittance to her sister. Juliet's hair being finished, she ordered Ann to undo the small mountain of mourning goods, and select the plainest garment. And, after all, it was with much hesitation, and continued wringing of hands, and moans and lamentations, that she allowed herself to be arrayed in these insignias of her widowhood. She more than once gave up her purpose, only as often to resume it.

CHAPTER XX

JULIET

Ann, having completed her mistress' unusual and oft-resisted toilet, received with surprise a message to convey to Father Duffy. She glanced at Mrs. Temple, to discover if she were really in her right mind. Upon this point she could not satisfy herself, for Juliet had buried her flushed face in the fresh handkerchief she had just given her, and added but the words: "go at once!"

Father Duffy, but little past the prime of life, was in the full vigor of energy and usefulness. A worker himself, he infused others with his spirit; droneishness wilted under the scorching rays of his perpetual activity, as weeds wither in the noon-day sun. He had accomplished wonders in his parish, and many another, less efficient than himself, might have supposed nothing more was to be done. Not so, thought Father Duffy. Literally and figuratively hills were to be brought down, and level places to be made smooth.

By precept, and still more by example, he taught his people to bear their burdens heroically, their prosperity with humility, their adversity with pious resignation. He had little patience with indecision, still less with querulousness and complaints. With those of his class, he believed that one's "first fruits" should be given unto God. One's best emotions, fullest love, highest loyalty, precious treasure. He had no faith in the piety of him, who, living in a costly dwelling, proposed to worship God in a habitation mean and contemptible; nor in that of her, who, clad in a thousand-dollar shawl, would drop a five-cent upon the plate of charity.

He was as quick to perceive, as was his will to act, or his hand to do. He saw at once through all sham and artifice. He could be almost said to perceive what was passing through one's mind, so quick was his discernment, so penetrating his thought. He might have been a Jesuit, nor fallen a whit behind the most polished and profound of that marvellous society of men.

Poor Juliet! To have sent for such a man, whose one glance could dissect her thoroughly! But, let us wait; maybe we shall have no occasion to repeat the epithet just applied to her name.

Juliet little understood, indeed, was incapable of comprehending the nature of the man whom she had invoked into her presence. Otherwise, she would never have sent for him. She had bestowed no particular thought upon him, anyhow; but he shared involuntarily in that measure of contempt, which she ever had cherished for Roman Catholics in general. She was not one bit in awe of him, nor felt less hesitation in addressing him, than she would have done in speaking to a merchant's clerk.

"I wish to see you, Mr. Duffy," she said, upon entering the little parlor, where she had met him the one time previously. The memory of that day, scarcely ten ago, came over her with such sudden distinctness, that she sank to the floor, beside the sofa upon which she had been about to seat herself, and groaned aloud.

"I fear you yield too immoderately to grief," said the priest.

"I can never mourn enough for John Temple," said the widow, disconsolately.

"Mr. Temple was a worthy man. We have all lost in his death; but we must not forget that he has gained."

"I forget everything but that I am wretched—the most wretched creature in existence. I hate equally the light of day and the darkness of night. I would take my own life, only that I have such a horror of death."

If the priest felt horror at her expressions, he did not evince it; but he said firmly:

"It is very wrong for you, Mrs. Temple, to speak thus. God does not afflict His children willingly, nor—"

"I am no child of God," broke in the unhappy woman, hiding her face in the crimson velvet of the lounge, against which she leaned, for she still retained her position upon the floor, in utter disregard of conventionalities.

"Though you may not acknowledge God, He is none the less your Lord and Master. Your will opposed to His is as smoking flax. He has seen fit sorely to afflict you, and you are utterly powerless. But, God does everything in wisdom. He has chastened you for your good, if you will but make a wise improvement of this dispensation."

"You talk as if you think I am a Christian. But, I tell you I am not, and never was. I know nothing about God. I have never cared anything about Him. I have lived without Him, and as though He did not exist. But, I am left alone now. I have nobody in Heaven or on earth. I am afraid—as if I were on water, and about to sink, or, as if the heavens were to fall and crush me."

"Yet God is near you. You have but to stretch forth your hand, and He will support you. Give Him your heart, and He will be a present help in time of trouble."

"But, I cannot find Him! And see, you do not tell me truly; for I put forth my hand, and it falls back wearily. I know—I do not expect to see God as I see a person; but they tell about Faith that is as good as sight; if I could only have that!"

"Are you willing to make sacrifices for that faith—what would you do, what give?" willing to test her sincerity.

"Do! give! I would sit in sackcloth and ashes! Behold me upon the floor: I would even sink beneath it, I would walk upon coals of fire, tread upon thorns, seek rest upon a rack of torture! And give? O, have I not been robbed of my all? I have nothing left to give!" and Juliet's voice died out in a mournful wail.

"But all this would not bring you to God, unless you yield to Him your heart."

"I have no heart; it is in the grave with my husband."

"Mrs. Temple, you will never find God while you cherish this spirit of selfish grief. Submission to His will is your first duty. Were you a Catholic, I could instruct you. I know not how to conduct a Protestant to God, unless I lead her in Catholic ways. Are you prepared to be so led? Or, madam, why did you send for me?"

Juliet hesitated.

"I hardly know," at length, "I wished for somebody who had been dear to John. He loved you more than all the world beside, except us, of course. He was so satisfied with his religion; his faith was so clear and full; he lived such a good life; and he used to say he owed so much to you. I thought if you could teach me as you had done him, if I could become good as he was, that I would learn of you, if you would take the trouble, even though you were a Catholic priest."

"You do not wish then to become a Catholic, really?"

"No; I do not. I wish to find God; or, to have such faith in Him, that I may believe as if I saw Him. Can you help me to that?"

"I can," replied the priest. "God has appointed me to bring souls to Him. He has appointed the way also, and I cannot go out of that way. I warn you, therefore, in the beginning, that while conducting you to the Heavenly City, I am not seeking to make of you simply a Catholic, but the convictions of your mind and the fervor of your heart will be of the very spirit of Catholicity. Are you still willing to persevere?"

"I am. I have no fears of becoming a Catholic. I can judge for myself. I can never believe in the divinity of Mary; nor in the worship of the saints and the adoration of their relics; nor in transubstantiation and miracles, and all those things; but you know what I want—and will you help me for John's sake?"

"And for your own. But you must have confidence in me. And first, you must cease to believe that Catholics regard Mary, the Blessed Mother, as a divine person; second, that they worship saints or their relics, and many another fallacy under which you labor. You must be willing to read and study, withdrawing your mind as much as possible from your bereavement, and giving certain time to the care of your children. In these matters you must be obedient, or I can promise no good result. Are you still resolved?"

"It is my last hope," thought Juliet, disheartened for a moment, and she bowed her head.

"You are sure you can help me," said Juliet, imploringly, as would say one sick to the physician, in whom were placed all her hopes of life.

"And behold I am with you even to the consummation of the world" passed through the priest's mind, and he answered, confidently: "Very sure, Mrs. Temple."

The friends of Juliet marvelled greatly, when it became known to them that she had sent for the Catholic priest, and was actually seeking to learn the religion of her late husband. For they looked at the matter in its true light, and smiled at her simplicity, in believing she could be instructed in Protestantism by any "Romish priest," how good so ever he might chance to be. Against her own inclination, but from the advice of her new friend, she occasionally received her sisters and a few former acquaintances. They went away commiserating her condition, as being semi-imbecile, semi-lunatic.

"She will get over this, go in society, and marry again," they prophesied. They were not the first false prophets who have arisen.

A year later, when Juliet Temple was baptized into the Catholic Church, these same people said:

"*They* will get her into a convent, next, where she will awaken to a sense of her folly." Another false prophecy, for Juliet did not enter a convent, though she had serious thoughts of doing so. Though she became not a Sister of Charity, in fact, she did in deed, and atoned in after years for the frivolousness of her early life, by patient self-denials and well-directed benevolence.

In the matter of Juliet's conversion, Father Duffy, as in every thing else, had done his work well. The widow of John Temple was no half-way Christian. She had put forth her hand in the way directed, and God had lifted her into the light. With her feet upon the rock of ages, she no more trembled under the impression of sinking beneath slippery waters.

She was not ashamed to be seen by her former fashionable friends wending her way to St. Patrick's. When she knelt at the altar to receive the bread of life, she became not "indignant" that any humble Bridget knelt by her side; for, dearer to her the most lowly person who now had received the waters of Baptism than any lady who rode in her carriage. Through the priest, it was God's work and marvellous unto all eyes.

CHAPTER XXI

"THE SPIDER AND THE FLY"

Both Leonora and Estelle wrote to their distant brother of the danger of his daughter. She was under the sole care of one who was fast becoming bewitched with the superstitions of Catholicism.

Startled and bewildered, Philip St. Leger wrote at once for his daughter's removal from the house of Juliet. During the few months remaining of her school-life, she should divide her time at the houses of her elder aunts. After that, she should take up her abode with her uncle, Duncan Lisle, at Kennons. This latter arrangement, which had been always understood, seemed now to all parties doubly desirable. She would be removed even from the city where Juliet Temple lived. For, of course, Juliet, like all converts, would not rest until she had made proselytes of all who should come within her influence. She had been much attached to her niece, and that niece was known to have had great affection and respect for her late uncle, who had been to her a father. Truly, great danger was to be avoided, and soon as possible. Althea was removed to her Aunt Leonora's, and forbidden to enter Juliet's house without permission, and accompanied.

Althea was now nearly sixteen; she had emerged from the

somewhat unpromising age, and had developed into remarkable beauty. Distinguished as were all the St. Legers for fine personal appearance, none had ever equalled this child of Della, given to God with that mother's expiring breath.

With the beauty of her father, she possessed the winning gracefulness of her mother, with the best mental and moral qualities of both. As a scholar, she excelled in all her classes; she had a real genius for music, poetry, and painting. With trifling effort she could execute most difficult pieces upon piano and harp.

"You have the hand of a master," spake Signor Lanza proudly, to this his favorite pupil.

"Il improvisatrice," was she styled by her admiring associates, whom she amused by the hour with her extemporary effusions of rhyme.

From all, you would have taken her to be from that land

"Where the poet's lip and painter's hand
Are most divine. Where earth and sky
Are picture both and poetry;
Of Italy—"

A Madame de Stael would have immortalized her as another Corrinne.

Heu, me miserum! Where shall we find goose-quill cruel and grey enough to write her down wife of Jude Thornton Rush?

"There are more things in heaven and earth, Horatio, than are dreamt of in your philosophy."

Have you forgotten, dear reader, that September night after

Ellice's funeral? How Duncan Lisle sat alone with Hubert, his child, before the bright fire, while the rain pattered against the pane, and the memory of the widowed man broke up into such a shower of reminiscences as almost, for the moment, to drown the fire of his grief? Do you remember that Philip St. Leger, returned from the East, came abruptly upon the scene, telling of Della's death, and the little child left at the North? Well, was it not natural for us to think that Hubert and Althea, children of Della and Ellice, the "Pythias and Damon" friends, should grow up and love each other, and marry at last, as they do in novels?

Yes, that was our pet scheme, indulged in to the last. But we are compelled to admit with the poet, that "best laid plans go oft astray." We are also compelled to think half wickedly with Amy—what pity it was Jude Rush fell down a precipice breaking his neck, thus giving his wife liberty to capture her own good master—and what pity it was too that Jude Thornton Rush did *not* fall down some precipice and did *not* break his neck before, spider-like, he had woven his fine web, and said softly to Della's daughter:

"Will you walk into my parlor?"

For, something like a spider was Thornton Rush. He was quite tall and too slender. His body was out of proportion to his long limbs, and his hands and feet had the remarkable faculty of protruding too far from every garment, even those the tailor declared should be long enough *this* time. The "ninth part of a man" would seize the sleeve at the wrist with both hands, give a good jerk and an emphatic *there*! But when Thornton Rush was ordered to lift his arm naturally, the wrist protruded like a turtle's neck.

"He must be made of gutta percha," soliloquized the discomfited tailor, giving him up as an incorrigible *non-fit*.

The rather stooping shoulders and long neck supported a splendid head for Thornton Rush. This was indeed his crowning attraction. Short silken curls of raven black clustered around it, shading a wide white forehead and delicately fashioned ear. He had a beautifully arched brow, heavily pencilled, within which a glittering black eye, too deep set, gleamed forth with unaccountable attraction. His nose was straight, small, but full of nerve. You would never guess from that handsome, firm-set mouth of his, where decision and resolution played about the cherry lips and dimpled chin, that he would have proved the coward and run from duty and from danger. No; but then Thornton Rush was made up of contradictions.

His mental and moral, like his physical organization, was full of angularities, discrepancies, and unharmonious combinations.

He could be gentle as the dove, but fierce as the tiger; kind and confiding as any child, but cruel and deceitful as Lucifer transformed.

So opposite qualities are seldom found combined.

The most brave men are often the most gentle; the most trustful are frank and open-hearted. To parody Byron's eulogy on "The wondrous three,"

Nature has formed but one such—hush!
She broke the die in moulding Thornton Rush.

What do you say? Althea and Thornton married and not one word about the courtship, that most interesting of all portions of a love-history!

It was the tragedy of "the spider and the fly" enacted over again. We would but shudder to watch that wicked, sly, patient tarantula, coaxing, flattering, urging the poor little fly, whose bright wings are singed with his hot breath, and whose wonderful eyes are held fast by the fascination of his scintillant, unrelenting gaze.

It is to be hoped, dear reader, that you are not of that kind who love to gloat over horrors. If you are, you must turn to some modern journal of civilization which is able to satisfy you completely. But Althea and Thornton are not married yet, they are only going to be.

After the lapse of a quarter of a century Duncan Lisle, for the second time, attended commencement exercises at Troy Female Seminary. Twenty-five years is but a dot upon Time's voluminous scroll, yet in that brief space has been crowded infinite change. Madame X—having retired from the school of education and from the stage of life, has been succeeded first by Madame Y—, and again by Mademoiselle de V—. More than half the young ladies who had graduated with Della and Ellice, who had looked like angels in simple white and blue, had lain down the burthens of life, and were sleeping peacefully here and there.

Duncan Lisle had not, for four years, seen his niece, and was not prepared for such startling developments of mind and person. He was proud to behold her queen of the school; queen, both in beauty and mental accomplishments. He too might be forgiven for one daring thought that soared down to matchmaking. It was not very strange that, remembering his earliest wife and only sister, and thinking of his one beloved child, the thought should cross him of the beauty and fitness of a union between Hubert and Althea. "I will send Althea's picture across the ocean to Hubert; I will write him to return home immediately," was the conclusion of this good father. All parents have such pet schemes, to greater or less extent.

The health of the master of Kennons had been for some time delicate. His journey North, undertaken partially for his own benefit as well as to accompany his niece to his home, proved rather injurious than otherwise. The excessively hot weather prevailing rendered the trip anything but agreeable, and he returned to Kennons much exhausted and debilitated.

He lost no time in carrying out his resolution with regard to his son. He wrote him a letter full of the praises of Althea, assuring him that the picture enclosed failed in justice to the original. He also spoke of his own failing health and his great and increasing desire to behold him again. Hubert Lisle never received this letter; it never left the office at Flat Rock; indeed it was destroyed at Kennons.

Thornton Rush had returned from Europe at the close of the war. Instead, however, of returning to Virginia, he had put up his shingle as a lawyer in one of the new States of the growing West. He had not forgiven his mother that she had allowed his several letters to go unanswered.

Two years had he now been at Windsor, among the wilds and roughnesses of a new country; still had his mother for him no word of congratulation, encouragement, or even recognition.

When Rusha Lisle read her husband's intercepted letter, thereby discovering his designs as to the hand of Althea, a new thought struck her.

It will be remembered that she took special delight in rendering others uncomfortable, and in setting up an opposition to everybody's plans. Against Hubert she had entertained a perpetual ill-feeling. Was he not the child of her rival? Should he win for bride this sweet child of sixteen, whose transcendent loveliness made an impression even upon her own unsusceptible heart?

Had she not surreptitiously gained access to her husband's last will and testament, wherein he had made his sister's child co-heiress with Hubert to all his estate?

What could be expected of Rusha Lisle but instant action to the following effect: First, to break her long silence to her son by enclosing him the picture designed for Hubert, and cordially inviting him to make her a visit at Kennons, where he would find the beautiful original.

Mrs. Lisle kept her own counsel, never intimating a wish or expectation of her son's return. Her surprise upon his arrival was well counterfeited; nor was it ever known beyond mother and son that the latter had not been first to make the overture. But this son, in some respects so like his mother, might have evinced less disposition to do at once her bidding had not the inducements held forth been all-sufficient.

Thornton Rush was not a lady's man. Byron was made miserable on account of the deformity of his foot. So our less distinguished but equally sensitive hero had always the impression that his long wrists and ankles were subjects of ridicule. He believed the ladies did not fancy him; he therefore made no efforts to propitiate their favor. If they happened to laugh in his presence—and the foolish things are always happening to laugh—he made sure it was at himself; and he shot at them most vengeful flashes from his cavernous orbs, which annihilated them not at all, but rendered them more risible.

"But there is a tide in the affairs of men."

"There is a hand that shapes our ends, rough-hew them as we will."

The inanimate picture at which Thornton Rush gazed did not laugh at him. On the contrary, it looked up to him with such a sweet confiding trust—O, there was something in that face he had seen in none other. It wonderfully attracted him. Even had it not, he would have made every effort to win Althea's heart just the same; and for the very reasons that had instigated his mother. He hated Hubert Lisle. To thwart him he would have circumvented heaven and earth. With Thornton Rush this consideration weighed even more than Althea's promised dowry.

Spite, revenge, avarice, every worst passion should be gratified in the accomplishment of a union with Althea.

Unfortunately, the situation of things at Kennons favored this wretched wooing. Duncan Lisle was failing rapidly, and had become confined to his room. Above all others, he loved Althea to be with him; but he knew, and upon this his wife enlarged, that she should be allowed considerable recreation.

When, therefore, Rusha Lisle came in to take the niece's place, insisting upon the latter taking a ride or drive, her uncle would join in the request, and Althea was compelled to go. Nor was it such a hardship. Thornton was ever ready to accompany her. And now, in presence of this guileless girl, he did, indeed, seem transformed. He was attentive, kind and gentle, he hastened to comply with her every wish, to anticipate all.

For the first time in his life, he put a curb upon his violent temper. He became kind, even to his horse and his dog— when in *her* presence. Discovering her taste for poetry, he sat up nights to commit to memory whole pages of her favorite Scott and Moore, Bryant and Longfellow, which he would repeat to her with exceeding force and appropriateness.

Thornton's voice was as contradictory as the rest. It could be soft or harsh, musical or discordant. To Althea it was only pleasant and gentle; and, by degrees, came to possess for her a wonderful charm.

Mrs. Lisle, so disagreeable to all others, had practiced remarkable effort and self-control in making herself agreeable to this young girl, whom she would fain help to draw within her son's meshes.

Mr. Lisle's first letter to his son, to which we have referred, was not his last. But every missive, more earnest than the former, met with the fate of the first. Every day he waited anxiously for the coming of the mail. It seemed all that interested him. It was pitiful to see his daily disappointments, the dying out of every renewed hope.

This constant alternation of hope and despair, with constant suspense, shortened his days.

He died suddenly at the last, his expiring gaze upon the portrait of Ellice that, as of old, still hung over the mantle.

Did Mrs. Lisle, in presence of death itself, experience no scruple in having kept the son from his dying father? Would she ever feel remorse of conscience in this world, or in the next? At all events, she expedited in every possible manner the wooing and winning of Althea. Was there in Heaven no guardian angel for this motherless child? Was not her very name suggestive of protection from above? Had Della's last prayer on earth failed to reach the throne of Grace and Mercy?

No obstacle appeared in the way, after the only one was removed by death. Thornton began to talk about a return to his northwestern home. His business would still further suffer by a more protracted stay. Already he had been informed of the *debut* of a rival, one Capt. Sharp, upon his own field of law and politics. A Captain for four years in the Union army—what a claim irresistible would that be upon the good will and votes of the people! What a tempting bait for the Republican leaders to throw out to the multitude of small fish!

But how could he go back alone, after having lived two months in the light of Althea's presence? So he pleaded his suit to the gentle girl, veiling still more his fierce claws with the velvet glove, realizing Shakspeare's

One may smile and smile, and be a villain.

Thornton Rush won his bride, and carried back to his northern home the young girl whose grace and beauty dazzled every eye.

CHAPTER XXII

ALTHEA

Several years have passed. We find Althea a matron of twenty or more, but did we not know her age, we might think her five years older. She has not lost her beauty; though it is of a softer, more pensive kind. She is a gentle, quiet woman, beloved by the people of Windsor, for she makes no pretensions, and they have no shadow of suspicion that she deems herself their superior. But it is a never-ceasing wonder to the good and discerning that she ever came to marry Thornton Rush.

Thornton Rush is a man of mark. He has his friends and his foes. To those whom he deems worthy of conciliating, will he fawn and cringe. Those whom he despairs of making his friends, or those whose friendship may do him no good, he alienates determinedly, and without scruple.

For four years has he waged a perpetual warfare with the Captain. The odds would have been against him, had he not in his wife possessed one advantage. While Mrs. Sharp possessed by nature the qualities expressed by her name and made herself unpopular to the good women of Windsor, Althea, without premeditation or effort, was a universal favorite. Thornton Rush was well aware of this advantage, and he made the most of it.

Like many another man, he did not like to come home and find his wife gone. He missed her as he would the sun from day. Althea was much inclined to remain at home; and Thornton would not often have found chance to grumble upon this score. He was not given to habits of self-denial; nevertheless, to secure good will and triumph over Sharp, he would encourage Althea to make frequent visits—nay, often insist upon it, against her inclination and his own private wish. If his wife could serve his policy, well and good. What was a wife for?

There were those who regarded Thornton Rush with positive fear. They quailed beneath the flash of his eye. Such dared not openly oppose him and were outwardly his friends. Some, lacking powers of penetration, deemed him better than he was, and thought there must be much hidden good in one who had won so sweet a woman for a wife. Few dared exhibit, or openly proclaim the intense disaffection with which he had inspired them. But those who did were bitter and unrelenting in animosity; were enemies indeed, worthy of the name. Foremost among these was Carlton Sharp. This Captain still led a company well drilled and faithful. On the other side, Thornton Rush, since about it was no smell of gunpowder, trained a goodly crew, with which he met the Captain's line. Victory was not always upon one side. Politics is a very uncertain *res gestoe*. And human nature, more uncertain still, would vacillate from wing to wing, now being a Sharp's retainer, and anon a hanger-on of Rush. Such changelings would not count, but that their vote weighs heavily.

Mrs. Lisle had already made one visit to her son, which lasted several months. During this visit Althea's eyes had been opened, and she had been led to wonder, as before in the case of her husband, for what purpose had been assumed the false garb of amiability during the time of her sojourn at Kennons. Both Mrs. Lisle and that strange woman's son were mysteries to Althea. To her mind of singular clearness and purity they were incomprehensible. Their falseness and hardness she was more ready to believe hallucinations of her own mind, rather than really glaring faults of character in them. Hence she strove to force herself to believe them better than they were. But this could not last—and at length the young wife was driven to the sad conclusion that her mother-in-law was not only harsh, unamiable, and unforgiving, but destitute of moral and religious principle, and that the man she had married was worthy such ignoble parentage.

Did Althea then learn to regard her husband with scorn and contempt? Did she become a woman's rights woman and inveigh against man's tyranny and woman's weak submission? Not yet. Althea was motherless, and to all intents fatherless. She had a warm, loving nature, and there were few in this world for her to love. She had given her first love to Thornton, and though she had become aware that it was not the deepest love of which her nature was susceptible she yet clung to him, shutting her eyes to his ill-disguised defects, striving to clothe him with the graces which she had at first supposed him to possess, and, insensibly to himself, refining and purifying by slight degrees his selfish nature.

Then Althea had a pleasant cottage, situated upon a grassy plain, and embosomed in native forest trees. She had her flowers, music, books, her day dreams and hours of inspiration, when she recited to the birds improvisations which might have thrilled or amused a more appreciative audience. Her naturally happy, cheerful disposition caught and reflected but the light, and dispensed warmth and harmony upon all around.

Althea had another grand source of happiness; it was in her

one child, Master Johnny Temple, now just passed his third year. With considerable likeness to his father, this child possessed the hereditary beauty of the St. Legers, with that peculiar, queenly poise of the head that had distinguished Della Lisle.

He was then a remarkably beautiful child, with a winning and loving nature. To keep him nicely dressed was one of Althea's sweetest cares; and the little fellow had such a proud air he would have been taken for a royal prince.

Strange would it have been had not Thornton Rush been proud of such a wife and child. But he kept his pride and admiration shut away from their objects. He never took the trouble to tell Althea that she was dear to him, even if he chanced to think so; reversely he had a sullen way of appearing to think his family a trouble and burthen. Had Althea suddenly died some day he would have been shaken into due appreciation; as it was, her presence was like the sunlight that flooded him unconsciously, and to which he was so accustomed he never thought to be grateful for it.

You have seen a little boy with a pet dog. What a life that dog led! Harnessed to carts, sleds, made to draw heavy loads, after his young master, besides jerked this way and that, scolded, kicked, cuffed—what wonder the abused animal ran away or gave up the ghost? Then the boy's grief! His dear, precious only friend that he loved so devotedly! He mourns, sighs, weeps, not dreaming that he has himself done his dog to death. He is lost, having no one to love and torment.

"I will not mind his cross words, his petulance, his spasms of anger," constantly repeated the patient wife, but they entered her soul. "I will disarm him with smiles and pleasant words," she every day resolved; yet every day was she pierced anew with his arrowy verbality. "He shall have to remember me only as a good wife and true," she said mentally, even while her heart was ground as with a heel of iron.

But the time was coming when Althea might not be able thus to fortify herself.

One August morning the family sat at breakfast. It was earlier than usual, for Mr. Rush was to take the boat, which was to convey him the first stages of his journey to his native Thornton Hall. Master Johnny was already up and in his place; for he was a wide-awake fellow, bound never to be left behind.

"Johnny will not eat; he has not been well for several days," remarked the mother anxiously.

"You are always borrowing trouble. It is too early for the child to eat," said the undisturbed father.

"His stomach must be out of order; he threw up yesterday all he ate," continued Althea.

"Because you stuffed him so. You are making a glutton of him. You ought to know he should not eat more than he can hold," replied Thornton, amiable as usual.

The child had put his chubby hands upon the table, and laid upon them his curly head.

"Look up here, sir," said his father, sharply, "what ails you?"

The child raised his head wearily, and looked pleadingly to his mother. She arose, about to take him in her arms, when the father interposed.

"Let him alone. The boy is well enough. You are making a

fool of him; he will never amount to a row of pins. I am going to take him in my own hands; he is old enough, and has been babied to death." "Shut up, I tell you," addressing Johnny, who was now crying for his mother to take him. "Yes, a new leaf shall be turned over just so soon as I return from Virginia. And you are about as much of a baby as he is, Althea," whose eyes he observed to be full of tears. "Here, another cup of coffee; you have no thought for me—you give all your attention to that child—there, there is the whistle now! Ten to one I shall be late, and all your fault, forcing me to talk instead of allowing me to eat. Hand me my valise—there, good-by and don't fret," and, rushing away, he gave no kiss to little Johnny, whom he was never more to behold; no kiss to Althea, whom he was indeed to meet again, to meet again and soon; but a gulf between him and her, insurmountable as death itself.

She turned to her child, now that there was no voice commanding, "let him alone." She rocked him in her arms a long time after he had fallen asleep. Her tears sparkled upon his jet curls, while her heart was heavy as lead in her bosom.

"Am I, then, so unlovely that my husband does not care for me? Once I thought it was so beautiful to love, and to be loved! His love is gone; and mine—O my God, let me not lose the last particle of love for the one I must live with until 'death do us part.' We might be so happy, but are so miserable! Is it my fault? My conscience is clear; it does not accuse me. He is so unhappy, so morose; he makes us all so wretched, when life ought to be so pleasant."

Althea had placed her low rocker upon the verandah. A gentle breeze stirred the vines that wreathed the pillars. The birds flew hither and thither upon boughs that shaded her cottage. The fragrance of flowers filled the air.

"How beautiful is all this visible world," exclaimed she. "How full should it be of enjoyment." "Yes, yes," chirped the birds, the breeze and the flowers.

She laid down her child, who still slept heavily. She gazed at him intently, resolutely banishing unwelcome thoughts of aught that should harm him.

The house was in confusion, as it ever is after a hurried departure. Althea busied herself with setting things straight. Then she sat down to her piano, and commenced a song; but her voice trembled too much. She changed into a favorite march, whose notes rose and fell like the storm-tossed billows of the sea. Battles, quadrilles, waltzes dropped from her finger-ends, as if they had been magicians, and so mingled, dislocated and inharmonious, as to make wildest, though still musical confusion.

Hand-weary, but heart-lightened, she took up a book. It was a new book, she had but half-read, "Gates Ajar." She came to the child eating her ginger snaps in Heaven; to the musician playing favorite airs upon the piano, to the dress-maker fashioning gossamer garments out of aerial fabrics, etc., etc. She put by the book.

"I do not like that kind of a Heaven. How could an authoress make a Heaven out of the lowest part of earth? To think of eating, darning and mending up there! We are to do in perfection there, what we most like to do here! The drunkard then will take his glass; but he does not go to Heaven. Wonder if the tobacco chewer enters through the pearly gates—'nothing that defileth or maketh a lie'—ah, how beautiful and charming Heaven must be; more than we can conceive, or she, who looked through 'Gates Ajar,' can imagine. I do not quite like to look through her eyes. I suppose my mother is there. How little I ever think of her—

wonder if she watches me from above; O my mother, my mother in Heaven, have pity upon your child!"

A noise from the adjoining room startled her. Had the cat gained entrance to her sleeping child? She went in hurriedly; Johnny was in spasms.

She seized him in her arms, and ran screaming for Mary into the kitchen. Mary ran for the physician, and the distracted mother, still holding the convulsed child in her arms, walked up and down the verandah, shouting for help.

Doctors and neighbors came. All that medical skill and friendly sympathy could suggest was done; but all in vain. When the spasm subsided, the eye was uprolled in unconsciousness, and the face burned with the fiercest fever. Then would come the fearful convulsion, and you would not know the beautiful face so racked and tortured. Again the demon would die out; but reason returned not from his relaxing hold. What a scene was there! All had been set in order a brief while before. Now, again, everywhere was confusion. There lay upon the floor the little cast-off garments. The child had done with them. His rocking-horse stood in the corner, his whip and gun near by, his box of marbles, his countless broken toys and the sled he had never used. The last time he had been to drive with his parents, he had seen that sled inside a store. He insisted upon having it.

"But there is no snow to slide upon," objected his father.

"Johnny no slide—Johnny have 'ittle ocken (oxen) draw sled."

So the sled was purchased, packed into the carriage, and that night little Johnny had wished to sit up all night to admire his treasure.

"These bufully flowers, mamma, see," pointing to the upper surface and sides of the nosegay, facetiously termed. At length sleep overtook him, lying under the table side by side with the gaily-painted sled, one chubby hand grasping the forward rung. The next day the sled had lost its charms, for Johnny was ill; and the next—alas, here was little Johnny! We might speak of Althea's bewildered grief; but why should a mother's hand attempt to write, or a mother desire to read what only a mother's heart can understand, and but imperfectly express?

CHAPTER XXIII

HUBERT LISLE AT VINE COTTAGE

It was all over, the death and burial of little Johnny. All Windsor mourned for the beautiful child and the desolate mother. Even Mrs. Carlton Sharp came, Mr. Rush being gone, and mingled her tears with the bereaved. And Althea was not ungrateful. She turned not away from all expressions of sympathy, as it pleases some to do. She knew that only kindness was intended, and to her wounded, but still loving heart, gentle words and deeds were as balm that is healing.

After the first few days, however, Althea was left more alone. The women of Windsor mostly did their own household labor, and the busy season of the year compelled them to remain at home. Althea could fix her mind only upon her lost darling. She collected his playthings, soiled, broken, and all. She gathered flowers to fling above the brown earth that hid him from her view. She wrote heart-broken verses in his memory, and many more she poured forth in unwritten music to the winds.

There was a certain comfort in thus being able to abandon herself to grief and lamentation. But how would it be when her husband returned home? What would he say to the death of his son? As was usual, would he blame her also for this catastrophe? Or, would this affliction soften his heart, rendering him more kind in his intercourse with herself? Althea was revolving this in her mind, in a measure temporarily diverted from her grief. She was sitting upon the verandah, amongst her flowers, herself the sweetest of them all. A quick step upon the path startled her. She arose hastily, and glanced through the vines.

A stranger that moment caught sight of her, and came around to where she stood.

For an instant, he remained regarding her; then he clasped her right hand in both of his, and pressed it softly to his lips.

Althea, taken by surprise, was about to resent such a liberty, when the stranger said:

"I am your cousin, Althea, you must have heard of Hubert Lisle?"

It was indeed, Hubert, just over from a six years' residence abroad. Had he been Althea's own brother, she would not have welcomed him with more profuse demonstrations of delight.

"I learned at the hotel of your great affliction, which must be doubly painful, your husband being absent." Hubert glanced searchingly at his cousin's face. He had vivid remembrances of Thornton Rush, and held the conviction, that however much he might have changed for the better, he could be still anything but an agreeable life-companion. He discovered nothing by his searching glance, for Althea was thinking of her child, not of her husband; and this reference replunged her into grief.

Hubert's sympathy was aroused, and he attempted words of

consolation. When he saw how worse than vain these were, he endeavored to withdraw her mind, by giving vivid descriptions of and experiences in foreign lands.

Althea made an effort—an effort for the lack of which died Dickens' Fanny, little Paul's mother—and listened through politeness and courtesy. Gradually, her mind awakened to a lively interest; and before the day was spent, she regarded her cousin as the most interesting gentleman of her acquaintance.

"How fortunate he should have come now, just in this time of my distress," she whispered to herself, as she was about to retire, stopping to weep over the little night-wrapper, whose wearer was gone, but which still had its place beneath her pillow. She had a thought, too, which she did not whisper, and it was this: "how fortunate too that he should have come while Thornton is gone, that no thundercloud may hang over us."

Hubert had made a short visit to Kennons. Mr. Fuller was still overseer of the plantation, which he had conducted satisfactorily. Mrs. Lisle had, of course, returned to Thornton Hall. Amy and Chloe were installed in their cabins of old, and had supervision of the white house. From these faithful servants Hubert had learned the deception that had been practiced upon his father, during that parent's close of life. At least, he learned how letter after letter had been written, how impatiently his arrival had been awaited, and with what bitter disappointment that father had quitted the world, unreconciled that his son came not.

These communicative old women unfolded to their pet young master, as they still loved to call him, the plan that father had cherished with regard to himself and Althea. For this also was not unknown to them. Duncan Lisle had dropped into Amy's ear more than one hint of this kind. He had none other to confide in; and during a sleepless night, while Amy watched, he whiled away an hour discoursing of his son, and of the project in view. This faithful servant had Althea's picture treasured with jealous care.

"You shall see it, Massa 'Ubert, an' see what you've done gone an' lost," unrolling the precious memento from its many wrappings, as if it had been a mummy embalmed.

Hubert beheld "what he had lost" first with admiration, then with a sigh. But the sigh was not for himself only; it was for what that sweet-faced soul must suffer, under such guardianship as that of Thornton Rush.

Hubert Lisle at once rightly inferred the destination of those letters which had never reached him; and he glared fiercely at the fireplace now filled with green boughs, that had afforded flame to enwrap aught so precious. O, cruel flames, to blot out two such privileges—giving consolation to a dying father, and receiving from his hands a wife little less beautiful or good than an angel! And more cruel than flame, than direful fate, than death itself, the heart of Rusha Lisle, which Hubert would fain have trodden into indiscriminate dust, in his first moments of grief and wrath.

An intense desire of revenge took possession of this outraged son; more particularly of revenge against Thornton Rush, whose duplicity in winning Althea was circumstantially detailed to him.

Hubert Lisle had not only traveled extensively, but had read and studied deeply. He had scanned all religions, from that of Confucius to Mormonism and Free-loveism, which is *beyond* religion, and had no settled faith in any. He had dived into German transcendentalism and metaphysics so deeply that he came out clogged and permeated as a fly miraculously escaped from a jar of honey. He was naturally good and true, simple minded and high principled; but unlicensed, untrammelled thought, unsubjective to God's law, had rendered him liable to erect false theories upon unsound premises, and had undermined in a measure that nice sense of right and wrong, which had been his proud, happy birth-right. Yet he would have been startled to have been told that he was not now, as ever, a bold lover of the truth, that he scorned not deception and hypocrisy and all manner of evil. He would have bounded, as from the sting of a serpent, from open temptation to meanness and wrong. He walked upon the border of a precipice, not knowing but he was upon the open plain. Thus walketh human frailty, when unenlightened by faith in God and unfortified by heavenly counsel.

A modern "reformer," self-styled, acting as a "spiritual medium," is said thus to have addressed a visitor:

"It is my very strong impression that you are my affinity. You are to be my husband; I am to be your wife. You must seek a divorce; so will I, and happiness awaits us."

Two divorces ensued, and the gentleman visitor and the "medium" became one, an affinity, according to "spiritual" directions.

Hubert Lisle would have turned his back upon such sophistry, and scorned such a diabolical medium, how fair soever. He had not, however, been at Vine Cottage a week, every day in the society of one whose situation so much appealed to his sympathy and kindness, when he became conscious that he had been taken into a high mountain, and had not strength to say, "Get thee behind me, Satan."

From this height was offered him a treasure worth more than

kingdoms and thrones and all the riches of the earth. Instead of shuddering and turning back, he fixed his eye upon the glittering prize.

"It is thine," whispered the tempter, "the hand that holds so fair a pearl is all unworthy. It chafes and frets within the cruel grasp which an ungleaming pebble might fill as well. It would glow in the sunlight of your fostering care. It would enrich your soul as a priceless gem; as an amaranthine flower it would breathe unto your heart an eternal perfume."

Hubert Lisle had made obeisance to feminine beauty in every land; but his heart had remained untouched. Like his father years before, he had arrived at the mature age of twenty-eight, unscathed by the blind god's arrow.

Hit at last, and so unwisely pierced! To love the wife of another! Hubert would have scorned such an insinuation but a few days before. But he had not then seen Althea. He loved her, was she not his cousin? He loved her, who could resist, she was so beautiful and good? He loved her, she was so unhappy, *must* be unhappy as the wife of Thornton Rush. She had been won with false words and deceitful ways and wiles. Thornton deserved to lose what he had dishonestly gained, and what he apparently valued so little. Had not Thornton Rush wronged and, as it were, robbed the dead, and bitterly betrayed himself to gain possession of a jewel which should have been his own, which he would have worn so proudly? Had not this man been his enemy from childhood; with his mother, the curse of his father's house? Ever in his way, a perpetual thorn in the flesh, could he not now dislodge him root and branch, and spit him upon an arrow, that should cease never to quiver?

Hubert Lisle experienced qualms of conscience, debated as to right and wrong, gave many thoughts to the censoriousness of the world, but he had not the fear of God before his eyes.

"I can win her if I will," was his confident thought at the first.

"I will win her at all hazards," was his later iron purpose.

And Althea! Oh! is it thus that the child of Ellice doth come to Della's daughter?

And what hath this daughter as a shield from the tempter? Came he not unto sinless Eve in Paradise; unto her even who had seen the Eternal Majesty, and listened to His voice?

And Althea had not laid up her treasure in Heaven. She had not given her wounded heart to Him who was wounded for our transgressions. She had not poured her sorrows into the ear of the Infinite, nor laid her bleeding hands upon the cross of Christ.

So turned Althea from a now unloved, ungracious husband; from a bitter sorrow for her lost child, to human love and human consolation.

But Althea was not won so easily from her stronghold of duty. Nor would she, on recovering from the shock of Hubert's first proposal, consent to flee at once, putting the sea between them and Thornton Rush. Hubert pleaded strongly and well, but could gain only this point. He would return to Kennons, and dispose of his property and hers. She would remain with her husband for the present. The first time he should raise his hand against her, as he had already done, she would leave his house and procure a divorce. With this was Hubert fain to be content; and the day before the anticipated return of Thornton Rush, after his absence of three weeks, he left Vine Cottage and the sad-faced lady who dwelt therein, confident that ere many months he would have Althea as his wife, and sweet revenge upon his old-time enemy.

CHAPTER XXIV

JEALOUSY

Naturally, Althea was a changed person in the eyes of her husband. A man less jealously disposed might have attributed this to the sudden death of an only beloved child. But to Thornton, the knowledge that Hubert Lisle, a man his superior in mental, moral and personal accomplishments, had associated with Althea during almost the whole period of his absence, this knowledge, we say, was to Thornton as gall and wormwood.

"And how did you like your cousin?" he questioned with assumed carelessness.

Had Althea answered equally carelessly, "Oh! very well," she would have aroused suspicion, for she well understood her husband. So she said with enthusiasm: "I liked him very much indeed. I wish you could have met him. He is very agreeable and most intelligent."

"You speak as if you thought I was a stranger to him. I have seen Hubert Lisle before to-day!"

"But you have not seen him of late. A six years residence abroad must have changed him greatly."

"Umph! Your cousin is not the first person who has crossed the Atlantic, as you would have me infer. At all events, he is a sneak and a coward to stay in my house more than two weeks, and decamp just before I was expected." Althea was silent.

"A sneak and a coward, I repeat; what have you to say to that?" demanded Thornton, his eyes blazing like coals of fire.

"Nothing," said the wife, indifferently.

"Nothing! By Mars! do you answer *nothing*, when I ask you a civil question? It is well he did not let me find him here; it is not the first insult he would have got from me, and perhaps something worse. If there's a person on earth I hate worse than Sharp, it is that self-conceited Hubert Lisle. He is a puppy, an upstart, vain as a woman, and deep and false as perdition itself."

He waited as if expecting a reply. None came; he glanced sideways to his wife, and continued:

"Yes, you two would make a very pretty couple, very suitable. Your two heads are forever among the stars. I wonder there is a book of poetry left in the house. It is a marvel you both did not sail away in some carved shell of hollow pearl, almost translucent with the light divine *des tous deux* within. For ottomans you could have piles of Scott, Moore, Byron, Shelley, and Keats; and for food and drink, you could have stringed instruments, and easel, palette, and brush. How contemptible are womanish tastes in a man!" Again he waited vainly for a reply. The pallid fingers of Althea were pulling in pieces a half-faded flower, upon which her lustrous eyes were unvaryingly fastened.

"Good heavens, Althea, how provoking you are!" cried

Thornton, rising from his seat and confronting furiously his wife, "cannot you speak to a man; what have you to say, what are you thinking of?"

"Thinking of?" she said absently, scattering the petals from her fair palm to the floor, then raising her eyes full to his: "Thinking of the fair little blossom that withered in its bloom. I have done wrong to weep for him such bitter tears; for he was *your* child, and had he lived he might have cursed some woman's life as you have cursed mine."

This was uttered apparently without anger, and in modulated tones. But no words of Althea had ever struck Thornton Rush like these. He was speechless; and when she arose and passed him by to an adjoining room, he stirred not hand nor foot. If she had expected then would fall the arranged blow, she would have been disappointed. But she had not expected it, nor even thought about it. The faded flower had, indeed, brought up her own withered blossom, as she had said. Had her husband's discourse been of Johnny, instead of the senseless tirade against her cousin, had he exhibited kindness, and generous sympathy for herself, she might still have been won back to duty. But now, Thornton's words and sneers, however deserved she might have felt them to be, caused her to contrast the wretchedness of a continued life with him with what it *might be*. Thus far she had been agitated by indecision and scruples, they should henceforth trouble her no more. She was fully resolved, even more than when she had promised Hubert.

In her own room, Althea withdrew the blinds and looked out at the sky. It was covered with clouds, save one space of blue.

"Thus is *my* sky covered with gloom," she murmured, "thus amidst the darkness gleams my one ray of precious light. O blessed ultramarine, from on high I take thee as a token. God is good; God does not will that I should suffer; He does not will that I should love a demon. I am still so young; a long life may be in store for me; a cruel, wretched life with Thornton Rush, who assumed the guise of an angel of light to win me to destruction. A peaceful, happy life with Hubert, for whom heaven itself must have intended me. The sin is Thornton's, not mine, nor Hubert's. On the contrary, to continue to live with Thornton would be a sin. I can no longer deceive myself or him, I love him not; I believe I could hate him!" and a gleam unusual shot from the large, dreamful eyes.

Althea forgot, while she thus soliloquised, that she could not thus have felt, or could not have spoken such words, had not Hubert Lisle won her love. While her heart had not been given to another, she could have endured her husband patiently, fulfilling her wifely duties, and possessing a conscience clear before God. She would leave her husband then, not because of the harshness and cruelty allegible, but because she had criminally strayed from her allegiance and given her love where she had no right to give.

So blinded, however, was Althea, she did not perceive this. While she was wronged, indeed, by Thornton, she was still farther wronged by Hubert. No unkind treatment of the one could excuse her for listening, without rebuke, to words of unlawful love from the other. They were an insult to her good sense and virtue; and so at first had Althea esteemed them to be. But by and by—ah, it is an old story, and the saddest, sorriest of all stories in this life of ours; reading it, or hearing it, one sighs that our guardian angel's wings are invisible, and that once from out their protecting shadow, we rush headlong unto darkness and death.

We will not assert that Thornton felt not the death of his only son; he was not so inhuman as to be unaffected. He would have given all his earthly possessions to hear again that winsome voice of his child resounding through the house. He had not realized

"How much of hope, how much of joy,
May be buried up with an only boy!"

until the house was darkened by the death of Johnny. The grief which he experienced, however, affected him strangely. As we have seen, instead of softening his selfish nature, it rendered him more morose and censorious. It alienated, instead of binding him closer to his bereaved wife.

One reason was in this; that Althea had for him now no winning ways. She made no effort at conciliation, and sought not to give or to receive mutual sympathy. Indeed, from the period of the conversation above recorded between husband and wife, he was like a volcano, and she like an iceberg. As much as he was capable of loving, he loved Althea. Desirable as had been her fortune in his eyes, he would never have practised such a series of stratagems and self-denials, had she not personally been of great value in his eyes. When won, and she was surely his, he discontinued his deception, and appeared his natural self. She became to him, as we have before said, like the pet dog to his young master, though secretly beloved, yet ill-treated, scolded and abused. The thought of her ever being lost to him had not occurred to his mind, until he learned of the visit of Hubert Lisle. With him, Thornton well knew he would suffer in comparison. That was the reason Thornton's mother had taken such infinite and dishonorable pains in preventing his coming to his dying father. Althea would surely prefer her cousin.

But Thornton was at a loss what to make of Althea's present behavior. He had at first felt a deadly jealousy of Hubert.

That emotion had almost over-shadowed his grief. But he could not learn that any communication was kept up between the parties. No letters came to and fro. The mention of Hubert's name caused no blush upon Althea's cheek. She spoke of him kindly and naturally, as of a brother that was dear to her. In the distant years, he had been convinced of Hubert's honorable nature. He might not have changed. At all events he was gone now, and might never return. It was more agreeable to attribute Althea's rigid coldness to a shock of grief, rather than to a shock of hatred to himself or of affection for another. Nevertheless, he gave her no peace nor quiet. He became angered if she did not converse, and equally out of temper with whatever she might say.

Does such a man deserve a wife? Let him have a woman, then, who will bring him to his senses—or what passes for senses—in a manner veritably Xantippean; and not one of those tender-hearted, peace-loving creatures who would bless some good man's heart and home.

There are few men upon whom kindness and gentleness will not make more or less impression; but our unprepossessing hero is of that unfavored few.

CHAPTER XXV

THE AWAKENING

After a few weeks, Thornton has something outside his house to engage him. Election is approaching. Although neither Thornton nor his rival are in the field as candidates, each has his favorite nominee to support. The fire that Thornton has kept raging within Vine Cottage is now transferred to hall, stump and settler's cabin. Sharp is not in the background. His antagonist hears of him, or crosses his trail here, there and elsewhere. He is put to his wits' end in checkmating and circumventing him. He, at length, learns something quite astonishing. He has returned from an extended trip to the country, supposing Sharp to be not far in front or rear. To his chagrin he has remained all the while in town, and been an attendant at the Catholic Mission, being held for ten days in Windsor.

"That is a game at which two can play, I am thinking," said Thornton, mentally, grinding his teeth at the thought of the votes Sharp's presence might secure among such a crowd.

"Althea," he said, excitedly, going over to his house, "that rascally fellow is robbing me of all the Irish votes. Get your bonnet and come with me down to St. Mary's. I can drop on my knees and become as good an idolater as that scoundrel of a Sharp. Who would ever have suspected him of pursuing that dodge? But he is up to all games. Come, how long does it take you to put on your bonnet and shawl? They say an old Jesuit is going to preach; I think when his mission is over, I will take private lessons of him in the art of intrigue. That is what Sharp is at, I'll be bound. Never mind your gloves; you can be drawing those on while we are walking along. You look like a charming little widow in black."

The wife looked up at the husband in blank surprise at so unusual an epithet as "charming" coming from his lips, and applied to her. But the truth is, Thornton had done an unusual thing—taken one glass too much, and he spoke unguardedly. He even drew Althea's little hand within his own and through his left arm on the way to St. Mary's, instead of striding on a few paces in advance, as was usual. Just before arriving, he addressed Althea:

"Now that you have come so far, do the thing up brown. Make your prettiest courtesy to all the graven images, and particularly to that idol toward the left corner. It will be no trouble for you to kneel; that is always in place for a woman. Keep your eyes open and bow low to every old lady who has a husband, or a son old enough to vote. Don't hold your kerchief to your nose, even should you be knocked over with the incense, and when the bell rings bow down double to the floor; ha! it is a wife can make or break her husband's fortune for time; do you hear, wife?"

"Yes, I hear," softly replied Althea, more than slightly disgusted.

They entered the church which was already crowded. But Thornton Rush elbowed his way up the aisle till he stood not far from the altar. A gentleman politely gave his seat to Althea, but Thornton continued to stand, a perfect spectacle unto all beholders. He folded his arms and glanced out savagely. The first eye he met was Sharp's. Yes, there sat his enemy, snugly ensconced in Mr. McHugh's pew—that same Mr. McHugh who had told him three days before, that he did not consider Sharp the honestest man in the world! He had counted on McHugh—and now where was he?

Protestants who were present were quite as much surprised at seeing Mr. Rush as were the Catholics. He had never been seen even in a meeting-house, unless at a lecture, political caucus, or some kindred rather than religious entertainment. Sharp was a rigid Presbyterian; but his rival had never thought it worth his while to pretend to imitate him in that particular. On the contrary, by keeping aloof, he found favor with the more numerous Methodists, the few Universalists, Baptists, Spiritualists, etc., which more or less abounded in the rapidly growing little town. To all these he could be all things. But as to the Catholic fold, ah, if that sharp wolf, or wolf Sharp, got in there would be mischief astir. He must leap after, for, to a Catholic, his religion was more than meat or drink, and he would become naturally a friend to him who was friendly to his religion.

Althea had but rarely been inside a Catholic church. When a child she had been more than once to St. Patrick's, with her uncle and cousins, during a temporary absence of her aunt. She had been partial to the Episcopal service; but as there was no society of this sect at Windsor, she had very often followed her husband's example of remaining at home on Sundays; though sometimes she attended at the different denominational houses, as inclination urged, or some stranger, man or woman, preached.

Upon this occasion Althea was peculiarly impressed; not so much by the blaze of light, the brightness and perfume of flowers, nor by the commanding attitude of the aged missioner, who stood grasping the mission cross and about to speak. It was the sudden memory of her uncle, John Temple, who so loved and practiced this same religion that touched her soul. He came before her, in all his simple, unpretending honesty and truth. Never so much, as at this moment, had she appreciated his worth. She did, indeed, bow her head with reverence before the altar, not in obedience to her husband's commands, but in tribute to her uncle's memory. She had named her only child his unforgotten name, and now the child had joined him in the spirit-world. The two came before her like phantoms evoked. Were they, indeed, hovering around her in this sacred place? Such was Althea's impression, and how guilty felt she before them! Still more lowly bowed her unworthy head, and pressing her clasped hands to her heart, she cried, "O God, be merciful to me a sinner!"

There was a hush in the swaying crowd, for the priest was about to speak. He had stood during several minutes, until even the latest seemed to have arrived; then, in the general silence of expectation, his voice sounded clear and full and his words were: "O God, be merciful to me a sinner!"

Such an unexpected echo of her own unbreathed words startled Althea like an electric shock. For a moment she raised her head, and her drooping eyes fell upon the utterer of that broken-hearted prayer. Then upon the clasped hands fell again the white forehead, nor was it lifted more until after an hour or two of stirring eloquence the missioner closed with a repetition of his opening words, "O God, be merciful to me a sinner!"

It had been to Althea the day, the hour of her visitation from on High.

CHAPTER XXVI

LIGHT AFTER DARKNESS

Mr. Rush was privately informed that his rival was to canvass "Stony Creek" precinct on the following day. Accordingly he was up before daylight, drank half a dozen raw eggs, for which he had a particular passion, mounted his horse, and left Windsor behind, before Mr. Sharp had opened his eyes. Before leaving, however, the politician shook his wife by the arm; there was no need, although, for she had not slept, and thus addressed her:

"Althea, I am going to 'Stony Creek' that I may head that fellow. Don't fail to attend the Mission to-day; and do, for goodness' sake, hold your head up, and not fall fast asleep as you did last night. You acted like a mummy. Don't know when I shall be back; you need not look for me. Have you heard what I said? Don't forget now about turning in with the idolaters, look at the old Jesuit, and pretend to hear what he says, if you don't."

Althea breathed a sigh of relief as she found herself thus unexpectedly left alone for the day. She would surely avail herself of the permission, command rather, to go to St. Mary's. She had not slept, nor felt need of sleep; she had never been so wide awake; indeed, it was as if she were just awakened from a life-long slumber.

While still meditating upon her pillow, the six o'clock bell rang; this reminded her that Mass had been appointed for that hour. She would go. She dressed hurriedly, and proceeding to the kitchen, told Mary, who was a Catholic, that she might postpone breakfast, and come with her to Mass. Mary looked up with a pleased surprise and cheerful "Yes ma'am," and was soon in readiness.

Althea understood nothing whatever of the ceremony of the Mass; nor, on this morning, did she seek to understand it. It was not for this purpose she had come to St. Mary's. It was to feel again a sense of that strange nearness to her uncle and her child; to feel again near to Heaven and to God. And, though her conscience had been painfully aroused, though she felt keenly a thousand stings and reproaches, which would probably but be renewed and heightened by this repeated visit, she would not have remained away, not though her dearest wishes could have been realized in an hour.

Althea remained absorbed in deep thought and reflection through the first, second, and third Mass; the quiet intervals were all the same to her. She was heedless of those who came in or who went out, as well as of those who knelt around the confessionals, except now and then to wonder, as she chanced to meet some tearful eye, if the world held another heart so lonely, desolate, hopeless as her own.

Hopeless? She recalled the day when she had beheld the space of blue in the sky—the hole in the day, Pug-on-a-kesheik, thus termed by her Chippewa friends—which she had taken as a token that her love for Hubert was no sin. She recalled the momentary joy that had animated her as she, in imagination, clasped that love to her heart, as a gain for her loss, as a balm for her bitter sorrow. She remembered how she had even dropped upon her knees in thankfulness to heaven for having given her such a comfort in the midst of her grief. Should *she* have scruples when ministers of God had lifted up holy hands and sanctified such unions? Thus had her first sense of horror been blunted, and blushless become her keen, womanly shame.

Why then, with a sense of the presence of the glorified spirits of her uncle and child, assumed that caressed infatuation, that which she had deemed a higher, nobler love, proportions of gigantic horror? Why had she spat out as gall and wormwood the sweet morsel she had rolled under her tongue? Why, giving up her only joy, trampling down with all her strength and might the one hope of her existence, had she returned to this strange house, wherein she could but beat her breast and cry out "unworthy, unworthy"? Was she the first woman who had mistaken dross for gold; and, finding her error, might not she, like others, fling it aside for the shining ore that lay in her path? Should her hand still grasp the piercing thorn, when the rose bloomed temptingly before her?

Thus listened Althea to human sophistry, until God spoke to her through the lips of the Jesuit priest. And he said, slowly and solemnly, grasping in his right hand the emblem of our religion:

"And unto the married I command, yet not I, but the Lord, let not the wife depart from her husband. But if she separate, let her remain unmarried, or be reconciled to her husband; and let not the husband put away his wife."

Had these words come down from the heavens in tones of thunder they could not have produced upon Althea a more stunning effect. Was she here to recognize the hand of God? Had *He* inspired this priest to speak upon a subject that was thrilling her with pain, doubt, and fear?

A masterly discourse followed upon the indissolubility of the marriage tie. "Shall it be insisted upon then, do you say," toward the close of his impassioned words, "that a woman shall suffer insult, effects of drunkenness, abuse of all kinds? This is hard, indeed, but there is something worse than that; for a suffering wife to break the law of God, and marry another husband! For, whether is it not better to suffer than to sin? Wherefore came our blessed Lord upon earth, but to save us from the effects of our transgressions? He laid down his life that we might live. He suffered that we might rejoice. But He suffered not the death of the Cross that we might enjoy to the utmost the pleasures of *this* life. He endured not the bloody sweat, the scourgings, scoffs, revilings, and all the attendancies of betrayal, trial, and crucifixion, that, with impunity, we might set at defiance His divine law, and live in open rebellion to the Christian rule He came to establish. God Almighty help us, if we expect to get to heaven in any other way than by the Cross of Christ! Think of it! The Cross of Christ! Can you associate with those words, so dear, so sublime, to every Catholic heart, aught of this world's ease, or luxury, or happiness? How many thousands saintly souls have flung aside all that the world could offer sweet and beautiful to embrace this hard, this cruel Cross! And meet they no reward? Hard Cross and cruel to eyes not comprehending, because separate from transitory joys, but yielding balm and incense sweeter and more as most closely pressed to the heart. And woman, first at the sepulchre, first in every good word and work, is it not *her* glory to suffer for the Cross of Christ? How much has she of His spirit, who cannot bear without rising anger one unkind word or provoking act? Who gives taunt for taunt, and blow for blow? Who disregards His express commands, availing herself of the civil law of divorce, which she knows to be at open variance with 'Let not the wife separate from her husband: but if she separate, let her remain unmarried, or else let her be reconciled unto her husband!'

"What is termed in Jurisprudence the common law, falls sometimes heavily in individual cases; but for that reason would we do away with it altogether? The law of the indissoluble tie of marriage does, we admit, fall heavily upon some, yea, many lives; should we, therefore, infer God's dictation to be erring, and practice the human law opposing His own? Supposing in some instances, a life to be made happier, even better; would that compensate for the abolishment of a law upon which rests the general happiness of domestic society—nay, upon which rests society itself? Better that few should suffer than that anarchy prevail. Better that all should understand the marriage bond to be indissoluble but by death, that it may be assumed carefully and solemnly as a life-affair of the utmost moment, and not entered into with thoughtless levity as a bargain that may be broken to-morrow. In a life-journey so intimate, patience, forbearance, meekness, long-suffering are requisite. These are Christian virtues which will render any yoke easy and every burden light. No Christian nation should legalize divorce. No true Christian will avail himself of the law of divorce. In the eye of every Christian man or woman, whosoever is married to him or her that 'has been put away' is one of whom it is said, 'they shall never enter the Kingdom of Heaven.' Be not deceived. Even though those called and calling themselves ministers of God blaspheme Heaven by professing to bless such unhallowed unions, they are of the spirit of darkness, and lead unto moral death.

"Were there but this life, the case would be different. You could live and be merry, because to-morrow you die. It is upon this principle the divorce law has obtained. The world and Christianity are at variance. The one offers you comfort and ease, the other a continual conflict with the flesh and the devil. In the end, the world's votary shall vainly beg for a drop of water to cool the parched tongue; while the Christian warrior, having lain aside buckler and shield, reposes under the green palms of victory and peace in the Kingdom of Infinite Love."

The noble follower of St. Loyola might reasonably find fault with the above, as a citation of his words. But they so glowed and sparkled that they could be caught only in fragments and snatches; imperfect as they are, we trust they convey an idea of what was impressed upon the mind of Althea when the Jesuit closed—"in the name of the Father, and of the Son and of the Holy Ghost."

Althea was stricken—not blind as was the persecutor of the Christians—but with a steady lightning-flash of light that was intensely distressing. It discovered to her her heart full of sin and shame. It betrayed the slippery sands upon which her feet were treading. It revealed the gulf into which she had been about to plunge. Upon such a flood of light she could not close her eyes. She reflected that Paul had cried, "Lord, what wouldst thou have me to do," and he had been sent to Ananias, the priest, "who would tell him what he was to do." She did not stop to marvel why the Lord had not Himself told him what to do directly, but instinctively did what Paul did, obeyed instructions and sought the priest.

It was now nearly noon. Althea had been sleepless, and had not tasted food since the preceding evening. She looked around for Mary, that she might accompany her to the priest's house, where she rightly supposed the Missioner to have taken up his abode. She saw not Mary, who had gone home before the sermon, supposing that as her mistress had had no breakfast, she must stand in need of dinner. Instead of Mary, Althea beheld Kitty Brett, one of Mary's comrades, whom she had often seen at her house.

Kitty Brett had one of the sunniest faces in the world; and it smiled all over with willingness as Althea made her request. O yes, she would go right over with her, and, if she wished, would introduce her to Father Ryan, the parish priest, whom she would at first be likely to see. Moreover, her mistress had gone to the country with her children, so she had nothing to prevent her remaining during the little time Mrs. Rush might wish to prolong her visit.

Father Ryan evinced no surprise, however much he might have felt, on meeting this unaccustomed visitor. Althea was in a state for no preambles and no delays. She at once inquired if she could be permitted an interview with the Missioner.

The priest hesitated for a moment. Had she been a Catholic, he would have put her off until after the laborer of the morning had been refreshed. Reflecting, he withdrew, and very soon after, invited her into another room, where she found herself alone with the true priest of God.

Oh! Althea, thy mother, who gave thee to God at the first moment of thy existence, and at the last of hers, who had aspirations for the truth which God may have regarded, must have wept tears of joy, and called upon the angels of Heaven to rejoice over her daughter that repented.

CHAPTER XXVII

ALTHEA'S TRIALS

Althea's conversion from error to truth, from premeditated crime, though she was criminal almost unconsciously, to firm amendment, was one of those miracles in which even Protestantism believes. Such Althea considered it—a direct interposition of Providence. She recognized, with peculiar awe, the hand of Almighty God, and became as a little child, willing to be led whithersoever He would.

It was natural she should turn to the bosom of that Church, before whose altar she had seen her own soul as in a mirror, and whose anointed priest seemed to have been chosen of God for her awakening and instruction.

A few years earlier, she might have had prejudices to overcome; though slight, for one brought up an Episcopalian. That her uncle lived and died a good and true Catholic, and that her embittered aunt had embraced and become greatly attached to the true Church, had insensibly recommended it to her confidence. At first, she deemed herself unworthy to enter the fold. She had broken, in thought, one of its stringent laws. What she had come to regard as but a venial error, now appeared to her as an unpardonable sin. So unpardonable, indeed, that left to herself, she might have despaired of forgiveness, and returned to it cherishingly, seven times worse than before. But this aged Missioner, wise and experienced, knew well how to guide this untried soul. She was not the first, by hundreds and thousands, who had knelt to him for direction. He well understood the malady, and like a skillful physician, knew what remedies to apply.

In a week, at the close of the Mission, Althea was ready for baptism. She had her catechism by heart, and was pretty well grounded in instruction. She had faith which would remove mountains, a confident hope in Jesus, and a willing heart and hand for Christian action. She stumbled not over Transubstantiation, nor Confession, nor any of the Seven Sacraments. She embraced them with a loving heart and a simple faith, not questioning but they were of God, since they were in His own Church.

Whispers and winks were on the increase among Protestants. To secure an election according to his own ideas, Mr. Rush had placed his wife where she had made her own calling and election sure. This fact was slow in dawning upon him, but when it had fairly caught his vision, it shone with the effulgence of the sun. His friends had no pity for him. He had placed his wife in the fire; what could he expect but that she would be burned? It did not alter the case that Mrs. Sharp had been also in the fire, but came out unconsumed. She was made of sterner stuff. Stubble would burn, but rocks were incombustible.

Althea anticipated a storm; but she braved it, and asked Thornton's consent to her baptism. She might as well have asked the mountain to come down and be bathed in the sea. He was fierce as the whirlwind, unrelenting as death. His words of scorn and anger poured down like a water-spout, but unlike this element of destruction, his fury became not spent.

He forbade her attendance at the closing exercises of the Mission, or any further discourse with the Jesuit. Of this Jesuit, he had jocosely asserted he was going to take lessons in the art of intrigue. He deemed the lesson had been given without his seeking, and it was no less galling from his secret conviction that it was all his own fault.

Had his wife asked his permission to join either of the other sects, he would have answered her with an indifferent laugh and sneer. *That* would have been of no consequence. She could have been a Methodist, or a Universalist, anything but a Catholic! Like a Pagan Diocletian, he would have gathered all Catholics together, and thrown them to wild beasts. The coming election had lost for him its interest. It had cost him dear. Everything might go to Sharp and the dogs; one thing was certain—his wife should not become a Catholic. He remained steadily at Vine Cottage, a Cerberus to guard his domain. The Missioner would leave Windsor on the morrow. Althea wrote him a brief note, which she sent by Mary, asking him what she should do.

His reply was this verbal message: "Wait—and trust in God!" Mary delivered this faithfully, and added:

"He said, ma'am, to tell you that he would never forget to pray for you at every Mass he should say."

"God will hear *his* prayer," was Althea's thought, and she was comforted.

The very spirit of evil seemed to have taken possession of Mr. Rush. He was more and more resolved to have entirely annihilated every trace of the new faith in his wife. For this purpose he sent far and near, until he had literally the proverbial "house full of ministers." His wife was under exhortation first from one, then from another, every hour in the day.

First the Presbyterian, then the Methodist, the Baptist, even the Spiritualist expounded and sermonized upon the several beauties of the Protestant faith. Their principal ammunition, however, was expended in besieging, battering and anathematizing the Catholic Church.

Every minister had a book for her to read, at home in his library, which he would bring her, the reading of which would prove convincingly conclusive. One had Fox, one Hogan, another Kirwan and Maria Monk, and still another the multitudinous tomes of Julia McNair Wright. As to Edith O'Gorman—no need to allude to this lately arisen bright particular star, in whose flood of light, the black sun of Catholicism was going down. Mary Stuart was not more tortured by Elizabeth's emissaries, than was Althea by these clever ministers. But the ill-fated Queen, nursed from childhood in the faith, was not more unwaveringly firm than was this six-days' neophyte.

With this array of ministers, however, was not her greatest trial. They might deem her stupid, obstinate, blind, and infatuated, but they were at least gentlemanly and polite. She could reply to them as she thought best, without danger of having her head taken off. She was even glad of their presence as they went and came again, because, while they talked, her husband was for the most part silent.

And when he demanded that one or other should receive her into his church, he was in turn offended at them, because they insisted that the lady's consent was necessary. When the subject was given over, and everyone had departed finally to his own house, then Althea's true martyrdom commenced.

"You have become a believer in Purgatory, and your faith

shall spring from actual knowledge; for as long as you live I will make this house to you a purgatory," declared the enraged husband, furiously. And he kept his word. But the good God, omnipotent on earth as in heaven, had said: "Thus far shalt thou go, but no farther."

Althea would have remained quiet and resigned, never mentioning the subject of her faith, but this Thornton would not permit. He would talk of it incessantly. To Althea it finally became a fire-brand, which, constantly waving to and fro before her eyes, threatened to turn her brain to madness.

She became dangerously ill. A severe fever had set in, to break up which baffled the physician's skill, when too late he was called. Thornton had persisted in not believing her sick, and had taken his own time for calling in Dr. Hardy.

Kitty Brett, finding a girl to take her own place, offered her services, which were accepted, as personal attendant upon Althea. As the unfortunate lady grew rapidly worse, Mrs. Moffat was engaged as head nurse.

This Mrs. Moffat was by many regarded as the salt that saved Windsor. Windsor would have gone to destruction long ago, physically, but for the saving help of Mrs. Moffat's hands. True, she was a married woman, and, like the martyr, was followed by "nine small children, and one at the breast," but this never prevented her lending a helping hand to any and every applicant. She could be absent from home a week at a time. The children could stir up their flour and water, and bake their hard cakes. They could lie down at night wherever they chanced to give up and fall, and arise with the morning's sun, ready dressed. Falling down cellar—it was a trap-door—other people's children would have broken their necks, but these little Moffats, after turning two or three somersaults, reached the bottom standing upright. They nursed themselves through mumps, measles, whooping cough, and all kindred diseases by playing in the creek; so that Dr. Hardy had serious thoughts of recommending "creek-playing" as a specific in such cases. They were hearty, hardy little fellows, all boys but the eldest, and cared nothing more for their mother's brief visits, after they had had their scramble for the *bon-bons* with which she was in the habit of regaling them.

Mrs. Moffat was, indeed, a most valuable attendant upon the sick. Unlike most people, she was in her element when in a sick-room. She could accommodate herself to every situation and emergency. If things and people did not go to suit her she could go to suit them. There was no grating, no friction where Mrs. Moffat was; her very presence was *oily*, so to say. She could lift people heavier than herself; there appeared no limit to her powers of endurance. She could watch night and day without the least detriment to her nerves. She could taste the most nauseous potions, and submit to most disgusting odors, nor make the least wry face about it. If she found a patient not very sick she would sit down and pour forth a gossipy stream of talk for an hour, when, ten to one, every ailment would be forgotten. There was a charm in her tone, word, and manner that affected like magic. Of course, this woman had a drunken husband—such women always have that affliction. There were those, even in Windsor, who said they did not blame Mr. Moffat for taking to drink—if *their* wives were always from home, and the house forever topsy-turvey, and the children making pyramids of themselves like a pile of ants, they should take to drinking too. But nobody could wait on these very people when sick but Mrs. Moffat.

Althea was sure of the best attention while Mrs. Moffat waited on her; and this capable person scarcely left her bedside. Kitty Brett was *her* right hand, as she herself was

Althea's. Kitty was kept upon a steady march, here, there, and everywhere; and she was as willing as was her superior. She could not do enough for one who had been persecuted for the faith.

The master of the house kept a steady watch over all. His argus-eye was ever on the alert lest, despite his vigilance, the Catholic priest should be smuggled into the house.

Althea was constantly delirious, and it was feared she might die without having recovered her reason. The crisis approached, and Dr. Hardy watched her silently for many hours. He had done his utmost, and though he hoped faintly he feared the worst. Mrs. Moffat's whispered loquacity was awed into silence. Kitty wept silently at the foot of the bed, praying fervently as she wept. Thornton had walked to and fro in his slippers, his long hands crossed upon each other behind his back, casting out occasionally fierce glances from his cavernous brows. He came and stood, like a thunder-cloud, by the Doctor's side.

"Any change?" he whispered.

The doctor shook his head.

"What do you think, any chance?"

The doctor looked at his watch, which he had been holding in his hand. "Yes, while she breathes there's a chance, I suppose," replied the doctor, without looking up, but changing uneasily his position.

"Well, I have an awful headache; I will lie down in the next room; if she is worse, you can call me," and the cloud disappeared.

Althea had been some time sleeping quietly, neither articulating nor moaning. Dr. Hardy watched her as only doctors watch their patients. It was more to him than a question of life and death—it was somewhat like the alchemist, trembling with hope and fear over his costly dissolvents.

At length, Althea's eyes opened, glanced hastily around and closed again. Dr. Hardy was not surprised. For the last half hour he had been expecting this, but he had given no sign. When her eyes again opened, he put some drops to her lips, which she readily swallowed. By-and-bye she gave a look of thorough consciousness, accompanied with an effort to speak.

Again, in an hour, she looked earnestly at Dr. Hardy, and moved her lips. He bent low to listen, and only himself caught her words: "Send for the priest."

Dr. Hardy frowned. Was this old anxiety going yet to ruin all? Couldn't she die or live without the priest?

"You are going to get well now," he whispered in reply.

"Send for Father Ryan, for God's sake," she again repeated, so forcibly that Kitty caught the words.

"I will go for him," she said eagerly, but the doctor interfered.

"No, I will see Mr. Rush;" for the anger of that man and his future hostility was not a pleasing prospective to the easy-going doctor, ever ready to propitiate.

Mr. Rush was like a lion, aroused from his sleep, in which he had found temporary oblivion of a torturing headache.

The doctor's words were not audible in the sick room, but Kitty distinctly heard the reply of Thornton Rush:

"I tell you I don't care. I don't believe it will make the least difference. If she has a mind to worry, let her worry; I won't have a Catholic priest in the house. I'll have the devil first. If she is going to live, she will live, anyhow. I have never thought she would die yet. For God's sake, let me alone, and don't waken me again, no matter what happens."

The doctor returned with lugubrious visage. But Kitty's was radiant.

She was seized with a thought or an inspiration, and she whispered:

"I will take all the blame upon myself; he cannot more than kill me. It is a good time—he has left orders to be let alone. The priest can come and go before he knows it," and she darted out without another word.

The doctor and Mrs. Moffat looked smilingly across at each other in the faint lamp-light, but neither made a movement for Kitty's detention. As the faithful girl had said, "the priest came and went" before the master knew anything about it. And Althea, having passed through her earthly purgatory, and now hovering, as she thought, upon the borders of death, had been baptized by water into newness of life, and been strengthened by that heavenly food, which is more and diviner than the bread of angels.

CHAPTER XXVIII

MYSTERIOUS DISAPPEARANCE

Althea was very weak, but continued slowly to recover. Several days elapsed, during which time Thornton's pain in the head had been upon the increase, and other alarming symptoms had been developed. These were intensely strengthened by the imprudence of a meddlesome neighbor.

Curtis Coe was Windsor's merchant tailor. He may have been more than the ninth part of a man in some respects; but when, under pretence of a friendly call, he informed Thornton Rush, already very sick, that the priest, Father Ryan, had baptized Althea—we say, when he did this intentionally and with malice aforethought, and with a sinful love of tale-bearing, and with utter recklessness as to consequences, he proved himself infinitely less, even than ordinary tailors of the proverbial size. He deserved the punishment of being hissed by his own goose.

The effect of this ill-advised news upon Thornton can be better imagined than described. What increased it ten-fold was the man's utter impotence to resent or punish what had been done. His ravings were fearful, his imprecations multiplied. Vain were the doctor's warnings that his anger would aggravate his disease. He continued to rave until he became unconscious of the words he uttered. To all in the house it was a relief when this man passed into unconscious delirium. One can listen to insane blasphemies with sorrow and pity; but only with horror and disgust to revilings, and railings sanely spoken.

On that night which followed Curtis Coe's wicked impertinence, two men sat up with the sick man. They must both have fallen asleep at one and the same time, for they discovered on coming to their senses, that Thornton Rush was nowhere to be found. The lamp was burning, even the fire in the stove had not died out. Having searched the room, they gave the alarm, and thoroughly searched the house, then all the outhouses, and finally the town.

All classes, friend and foe, were aroused. A general panic prevailed. Each one considered himself in danger, while Thornton Rush, as a lunatic, was at large. Posters were sent abroad and telegrams announced the mysterious disappearance to neighboring villages and cities. The river was dragged, old cellars and wells were dived into.

Windsor had at length a mystery, and it was an appalling one. People began to canvass it in whisper. A suspicion began to be bruited around. We do not affirm that Mrs. Moffat originated this suspicion, but she whispered it about from house to house. It was to this strange effect, the Catholics had formed a league and spirited away this enemy of their faith. Kitty Brett had boldly set his words at defiance, and the priest had boldly entered the house he had been forbidden, and baptized and anointed, and practiced what other witcheries he had no business.

If Kitty would do this much, and if Father Ryan would do that much, why, what was there they would *not* do?

This view of the case accounted for the wise solemnity prevailing among the Catholics generally. They were observed to purse up their mouths, and shake their heads; and one old patriarch had been heard to say that the Evil One had got his own. Why should he say that, if he did not know something about it?

It became another Morgan affair. Women began to turn off Catholic servant girls. There was a strong talk of discharging every Irishman from the Mills and Railroad. A continual espionage upon the movements of the Catholics was kept up. Traps were laid for self-committal. Bribes were offered and promises of security to any who would turn State's evidence. Threats were made here and there that leading Catholics should be arrested; at all events, the ringleader should be made to suffer. All seemed to settle down upon that Father Ryan must necessarily have been the aider and abettor, if not the suggestor, in such a high-handed proceeding. It mattered not, that during his five years' stay at Windsor, he had lived peaceably and orderly, and set a good example. All that served but a cloak to just such deeds as this kidnapping of a respectable citizen.

This whirlwind of talk, however, amounted to nothing more. The Catholic population was getting stronger every day; it was surprising how many new families kept pouring in. So it happened no one dared lay hands on Father Ryan.

Autumn passed into winter, and winter merged into spring, still no trace had been discovered of the missing man.

Althea had entirely recovered the health and bloom of youth. She was never more beautiful than now, at the still early age of twenty-two. She had mourned for her husband only as for a soul that was lost. She believed he must have perished in some strange way, and her daily prayer was that the manner of his death might some time be brought to light. The good God had snatched herself from the verge of the grave. He had said unto her, through his servant, "wait, and trust in God," and God had delivered her out of her troubles. She lived alone at Vine Cottage, the faithful Kitty her servant and companion.

CHAPTER XXIX

HUBERT'S SECOND VISIT

In June, the month of roses, came Hubert Lisle to visit Althea. He came thus early in her presumed widowhood, to woo her for his wife. But she would not hear one word of love from his lips. She had studied her religion, and found that its laws forbade marriage with another until abundant proof had been obtained of the death of her husband. So far, she had but proof presumptive. He had disappeared at such a time and in such a state as, to most minds, forbade even a possibility that he should have continued to exist. Again, the Catholic rule forbade the marriage of cousins.

Hubert urged to this that they were not strictly cousins. His father and her mother were but half-brother and sister.

Again, the Catholic Church did not forbid, but strongly discountenanced the marriage of a Catholic with a Protestant. She, Althea, loved her Church so well, she would not do that which the Church disapproved.

These were three great obstacles in the way then, to his marriage with Althea, Hubert found. He began to think he had now a more formidable opponent in the Church than he had had in Thornton Rush. He had succeeded in winning from Althea a promise to sue for a divorce. The rest would be easy. But he found it impossible, with all his eloquence, to prevail upon her to take one step contrary even to the wish of this more tyrannical guardian. He even went to the priest. He had seen Father Ryan at Mass, for, of course, he accompanied his cousin. He judged from his open, honest face that it would be an easy matter to win him over to his views. He entered upon the subject confidently, but ended very much discomfited. Father Ryan would listen to but one point, which was that Althea was not at liberty to entertain thoughts of marriage until conclusive proof was obtained of her husband's death. Hubert reverting to the other points— "All that comes afterward," was all the priest would say.

"But, supposing nothing more is ever heard of Thornton Rush, which is almost certain, is Althea to live a widow to the end of her days?" questioned Hubert incredulously.

"Yes," replied the priest. "And allow me to intimate," he continued gently, "that, entertaining the dispositions you do, it is improper you should remain a guest at Vine Cottage. As a cousin you were privileged, perhaps, according to your Protestant views, but as you are a suitor, it is quite different."

Having politely listened to these words of the priest, he wisely made up his mind to take his leave, before he should hear them reiterated from the lips of Althea.

"Well, cousin," presenting himself before her, on returning from the priest's, "I have had the courage, or the impudence, to consult Father Ryan; he is as inexorable as yourself. It is astonishing with what an iron will this Catholic faith infuses people. Last fall you promised to marry me, although a thousand difficulties were to be overcome. Now, that you are your own mistress, according to every human probability, and you are at perfect liberty, free from any scruples about the right and wrong of the thing, and yet—and yet how strange! You have scruples more binding a hundred fold. And Father Ryan, the gentlest, quietest person, whom you would not believe could say *no*, whom I made sure I could prevail upon to intercede for me, is just as resolute as Napoleon, as unyielding as Draco. What does it mean? Is it in the religion or what?"

"I believe, Hubert, it is the love of God in the heart. We love God better than the world, or aught the world can offer. We love God so well, that we fear to break His holy law," replied Althea.

"But others love God too, who are not Catholics, but they are not so inexorably bound."

"They have not the restraints of the Church. They have not its laws to govern them, its teachings to instruct, its pastors to guide and direct. Moreover, they cannot expect heavenly graces in abundance who are out of the true Church. Christ's promise of assistance is to His Church, His anathema against those who will not hear it."

"It looks to me as though you had taken upon yourself a yoke, and the bonds of servitude," Hubert remarked disconsolately.

"The bonds of the dear Lord Jesus, yes," and Althea's countenance glowed with enthusiasm.

"But Christian bonds should not press so heavily. Protestants in all these things do as they please, yet they profess to be bound with the same fetters."

"Profess! what use in professing when every day they burst them asunder as would they gossamer threads? I assure you,

Hubert, that is one of the beauties of the Catholic Church. Its laws are so binding, its teachings so direct, its discipline so perfect, that one cannot stray away blindly. The obedient child who would be pained not to do the Father's will is kept in the straight and narrow way, the light is held steadily before his eyes; if he stumble or turn aside he is brought back, and if he become restive and the 'fetters,' grateful to the loving child, bind too galling he throws them off, more willing to be lost than bear self-denial for the present. For myself, Hubert, I have started for heaven, confident of arriving if I follow the path marked out for me. If I do not follow in that path I have no hope but of straying far from that desired haven, the happy land of souls."

"Althea, I believe you have never loved me," suddenly exclaimed Hubert, steadily regarding his cousin.

"That is a cruel assertion, and it wounds me more than you can think," returned the lady, deeply moved. "Would I could forget that I ever loved you! The memory recalls my sin, my shame, and, thank God, my repentance. I deserve that you should recall all this to me, but I pray you, if you have regard for me, never to refer to this again."

"Forgive me, Althea, I did not intend thus to pain you. You are right and I am wrong. While regretting, I honor you the more for the noble stand you have taken. I go, Althea, and should I ever come again, you shall behold me worthier, God willing. I shall think of you as resting under the very shadow of heaven, and no ill, I am sure, will betide you. Farewell, and God will help you."

CHAPTER XXX

"AND THE SEA SHALL GIVE UP ITS DEAD"

The summer at Windsor was an unprecedently hot one. No rain in July, no rain in August, and September's sun was shining fiercely down upon parched earth, dried up rivers, panting animals, and complaining men. There would be no wheat, no corn; potatoes were dwarfed, and vegetables literally dried and hardened. Grass would be light, and cattle would be starved, if not first choked with thirst. The heavens were as brass, the fiery atmosphere like that of a furnace. Was there about to be a general conflagration, "when the earth and the heavens should be rolled together as a scroll?"

The great Mississippi was never so low. Inquiring urchins made explorations up and down the dried banks with all the enthusiasm of explorers of the Nile. Even the women of Windsor proposed a bold feat. This was none other than in a body to ford the Mississippi. It would be something worth telling of, when, after some flood, the river should widen to the space of a mile.

Accordingly, old calico wrappers were brought into requisition, and a small army of women stood upon the shores. You might have thought from the voices of fear, hesitation, reproach, and encouragement, another Red Sea was before them, and behind them a Pharaoh's host. All the women of Windsor were not engaged in this expedition. Some were milking cows, and some were putting dear little children to sleep; some were preparing late suppers for dilatory husbands, and not a few were gathered together in knots, discussing the impropriety and scandal of such a bold proceeding.

Our heroine at Vine Cottage, entirely unaware of the movement, was enjoying the twilight in playing soft airs upon the piano.

To one uninformed, a pow-wow of Indians might have been supposed to be going on. There were shrieks and wails, and screams of laughter, and cries of terror. There were threatenings, scoldings, and coaxings. Were all the grammars in the world made up of interjections they could scarcely have contained the list that rent the air, between the two Mississippi shores, upon that eventful night. The heavens were still above, though they might have been supposed to have disappeared entirely, so loudly and fervently were they invoked.

"Why, it is enough to raise the dead," exclaimed a solitary traveler, a stranger in town, perambulating a neighboring bluff.

As the vociferating army neared the opposite shore, there was a momentary silence; that breathless silence which precedes the storm. Then uprose such a terrific scream, such a commingled shout of horror, as only frightened women can give vent to. This brought men, women and children in throngs to the scene. Some leaped into boats, some walked in to the rescue. The majority awaited ashore the unfolding of events.

Mrs. Sharp had caught her foot in something as she was about to ascend the opposite bank. In attempting to save herself, she fell with her hands upon the soggy substance that had intercepted her. She was a thorough-going woman, and determined to ascertain what lay like a log in her path, the water scarcely covering it. She prevailed upon two or three to assist her in dragging it upward partially to the dim light— when lo! within a saturated, slimy bed-comforter was a human form! It was brought across to Windsor, officials summoned, and, despite decomposition and fearful change, recognized to be the remains of Thornton Rush! There was great sensation, and a faint revival of whispers about his having been spirited away to his death by Popish emissaries; but these soon died, for want of breath, as the Irishman would say.

The death of Mr. Rush was, by the majority, accounted for naturally. In his delirium he had strayed he knew not whither. He had grasped the heavy quilt tightly around him, which, held firmer in the clasp of the dead, had filled with water, and prevented the body from rising.

It seemed unaccountable that when the river was dragged it should not have been discovered: are not mysteries, however, every day transpiring before our eyes, about which we marvel in vain?

CHAPTER XXXI

CONCLUSION

To-day, Althea is the happy wife of Hubert Lisle and the honored mistress of Kennons, which is bright and beautiful again with sweet woman's presence.

Two obstacles to the union of Hubert and Althea had disappeared. She had been proved to be matrimonially free, and he had become, from study and conviction, a full believer in her faith, of which he made open profession. The fact that they were cousins still remained. As there were considerable delays in the consummation of the marriage, it was doubtless owing to the smoothing away of this difficulty. And as both parties hold the Holy Father in most grateful and loving remembrance, and their most cherished design is to make him a visit at his prison in the Vatican, it is probable that a dispensation from Rome severed the last link of obstruction, and permitted Father Ryan, willingly at last, to tie the Gordion Knot.

Arriving at Kennons, Althea, of course, paid her respects to Mrs. Lisle at Thornton Hall. She found her in a deplorable situation. A seated cancer upon the face was eating away her life, as it had already destroyed every vestige of her former beauty.

She had great difficulty in prevailing upon servants to attend her. She was so irritable and so offensive that even money could not purchase aid.

And what did Althea? Sacrificed every ill-feeling, overcame repulsion, put up with taunts and cross words, and waited on Thornton Rush's mother as if she had been her own. And this in the happy beginning of her wedded life with Hubert Lisle. And what reward had she? None in this life, save the consciousness of having struggled to overcome nature, to render good for evil, and to perform that loving charity which our Saviour commended in the Samaritan, and ever inculcates in His Church.

Notwithstanding Althea's patient, persistent efforts, Rusha Lisle, having hardened her heart, died in her sins.

To Althea, who stood above her dying bed, she whispered hoarsely:

"You have done all this for the sake of my property. I understood all. You will find out I wasn't fooled up to the last. You couldn't cheat me with your quiet, gentle ways; ha! ha!" and the wretched woman went out in the night of death, comprehending not the sweet, Christian life of such as Althea, but believing all natures dark and cruel as her own. It was from her own she drew her judgment of another.

She had bequeathed all her property to an idle cousin, whom it will but accelerate in his downward course of idleness and dissipation.

Arrangements had all been made for a visit to Europe, and particularly to Rome, as soon as possible after Mrs. Lisle's death. Here, again, was a disappointment.

Letters were received from Turkey, from the hand of Althea's father. He had lost his second wife, Emily Dean. He was about to sail for America, and should bring his two youngest children, little girls, aged respectively six and eight, whom he hoped Althea would make room for in her new home. He was unable to embark as soon as was intended, and arrived six weeks later than was designed.

Philip St. Leger, then, arrived once more at Kennons. His hair was silvery white. He was firm, erect, and still very fine looking. It was a sad place, however, for the Missionary, who began to feel the world to be receding from his grasp.

He talked with Hubert, somewhat at length, upon the subject of his religion. To Althea he made no allusion concerning it. He, doubtless, judged her to have become as infatuated, and "wedded to her idols" as he had found to be his sister, Juliet. He could not help from perceiving, blind as he was, that there was a very great change for the better in this same sister, whose folly and levity he well remembered.

He soon returned to Turkey, accompanied by a third wife. This time, Mrs. St. Leger was not a pupil from the famous seminary. Philip had acquired wisdom, perhaps, with time, and was glad to take a maiden lady of forty acknowledged years, who was a most amiable, warm-hearted woman by the name of Snow, Lucy being her first name. Success to Philip and his bride as they sail across the seas, nearing that grand sea that rolls around all the world! Their own disappointments have met Hubert and Althea. But these have no power to disturb their patience and serenity. They have established schools for the whites and the blacks on their estate, and are teaching the doctrines and practices of the new Faith.

The cars run through Flat Rock. This point has become quite a town, and a small Catholic church tells by its cross and altar that the true faith hath found its way thither. To this church come Hubert and Althea, Sundays and holidays. Maria and Frances, Althea's young sisters, come with them; for it was only upon this condition that Hubert would receive them. That Philip St. Leger should have consented to this, proves that a change has come over him since a score of years. Kitty Brett is Althea's faithful attendant. She chose to leave all her friends, rather than be separated from the woman whose life she had helped to save.

Amy and Chloe, old cronies, as they term themselves, look bright and young again, along with Kennon's rejuvenation. They hold long discourses over their pipes and snuff about the past and present, their deepest regret being that Master Duncan could not have lived to see this realization of his dearest wishes.

Every Sunday they go and sprinkle his grave and that of Ellice with holy water. They kneel by the cross which Hubert and Althea have planted, and, folding piously their homely hands, thank God for the return of the one, the gift of the other, and for the Cross, and the Light, and the Crown they have brought with them to dear old Kennons.

Choose from Thousands of 1stWorldLibrary Classics By

A. M. Barnard
Ada Leverson
Adolphus William Ward
Aesop
Agatha Christie
Alexander Aaronsohn
Alexander Kielland
Alexandre Dumas
Alfred Gatty
Alfred Ollivant
Alice Duer Miller
Alice Turner Curtis
Alice Dunbar
Allen Chapman
Alleyne Ireland
Ambrose Bierce
Amelia E. Barr
Amory H. Bradford
Andrew Lang
Andrew McFarland Davis
Andy Adams
Angela Brazil
Anna Alice Chapin
Anna Sewell
Annie Besant
Annie Hamilton Donnell
Annie Payson Call
Annie Roe Carr
Annonaymous
Anton Chekhov
Archibald Lee Fletcher
Arnold Bennett
Arthur C. Benson
Arthur Conan Doyle
Arthur M. Winfield
Arthur Ransome
Arthur Schnitzler
Arthur Train
Atticus
B.H. Baden-Powell
B. M. Bower
B. C. Chatterjee
Baroness Emmuska Orczy
Baroness Orczy
Basil King
Bayard Taylor
Ben Macomber
Bertha Muzzy Bower
Bjornstjerne Bjornson

Booth Tarkington
Boyd Cable
Bram Stoker
C. Collodi
C. E. Orr
C. M. Ingleby
Carolyn Wells
Catherine Parr Traill
Charles A. Eastman
Charles Amory Beach
Charles Dickens
Charles Dudley Warner
Charles Farrar Browne
Charles Ives
Charles Kingsley
Charles Klein
Charles Hanson Towne
Charles Lathrop Pack
Charles Romyn Dake
Charles Whibley
Charles Willing Beale
Charlotte M. Braeme
Charlotte M. Yonge
Charlotte Perkins Stetson
Clair W. Hayes
Clarence Day Jr.
Clarence E. Mulford
Clemence Housman
Confucius
Coningsby Dawson
Cornelis DeWitt Wilcox
Cyril Burleigh
D. H. Lawrence
Daniel Defoe
David Garnett
Dinah Craik
Don Carlos Janes
Donald Keyhoe
Dorothy Kilner
Dougan Clark
Douglas Fairbanks
E. Nesbit
E. P. Roe
E. Phillips Oppenheim
E. S. Brooks
Earl Barnes
Edgar Rice Burroughs
Edith Van Dyne
Edith Wharton

Edward Everett Hale
Edward J. O'Biren
Edward S. Ellis
Edwin L. Arnold
Eleanor Atkins
Eleanor Hallowell Abbott
Eliot Gregory
Elizabeth Gaskell
Elizabeth McCracken
Elizabeth Von Arnim
Ellem Key
Emerson Hough
Emilie F. Carlen
Emily Bronte
Emily Dickinson
Enid Bagnold
Enilor Macartney Lane
Erasmus W. Jones
Ernie Howard Pie
Ethel May Dell
Ethel Turner
Ethel Watts Mumford
Eugene Sue
Eugenie Foa
Eugene Wood
Eustace Hale Ball
Evelyn Everett-green
Everard Cotes
F. H. Cheley
F. J. Cross
F. Marion Crawford
Fannie E. Newberry
Federick Austin Ogg
Ferdinand Ossendowski
Fergus Hume
Florence A. Kilpatrick
Fremont B. Deering
Francis Bacon
Francis Darwin
Frances Hodgson Burnett
Frances Parkinson Keyes
Frank Gee Patchin
Frank Harris
Frank Jewett Mather
Frank L. Packard
Frank V. Webster
Frederic Stewart Isham
Frederick Trevor Hill
Frederick Winslow Taylor

Friedrich Kerst
Friedrich Nietzsche
Fyodor Dostoyevsky
G.A. Henty
G.K. Chesterton
Gabrielle E. Jackson
Garrett P. Serviss
Gaston Leroux
George A. Warren
George Ade
Geroge Bernard Shaw
George Cary Eggleston
George Durston
George Ebers
George Eliot
George Gissing
George MacDonald
George Meredith
George Orwell
George Sylvester Viereck
George Tucker
George W. Cable
George Wharton James
Gertrude Atherton
Gordon Casserly
Grace E. King
Grace Gallatin
Grace Greenwood
Grant Allen
Guillermo A. Sherwell
Gulielma Zollinger
Gustav Flaubert
H. A. Cody
H. B. Irving
H.C. Bailey
H. G. Wells
H. H. Munro
H. Irving Hancock
H. R. Naylor
H. Rider Haggard
H. W. C. Davis
Haldeman Julius
Hall Caine
Hamilton Wright Mabie
Hans Christian Andersen
Harold Avery
Harold McGrath
Harriet Beecher Stowe
Harry Castlemon
Harry Coghill
Harry Houidini

Hayden Carruth
Helent Hunt Jackson
Helen Nicolay
Hendrik Conscience
Hendy David Thoreau
Henri Barbusse
Henrik Ibsen
Henry Adams
Henry Ford
Henry Frost
Henry James
Henry Jones Ford
Henry Seton Merriman
Henry W Longfellow
Herbert A. Giles
Herbert Carter
Herbert N. Casson
Herman Hesse
Hildegard G. Frey
Homer
Honore De Balzac
Horace B. Day
Horace Walpole
Horatio Alger Jr.
Howard Pyle
Howard R. Garis
Hugh Lofting
Hugh Walpole
Humphry Ward
Ian Maclaren
Inez Haynes Gillmore
Irving Bacheller
Isabel Cecilia Williams
Isabel Hornibrook
Israel Abrahams
Ivan Turgenev
J.G.Austin
J. Henri Fabre
J. M. Barrie
J. M. Walsh
J. Macdonald Oxley
J. R. Miller
J. S. Fletcher
J. S. Knowles
J. Storer Clouston
J. W. Duffield
Jack London
Jacob Abbott
James Allen
James Andrews
James Baldwin

James Branch Cabell
James DeMille
James Joyce
James Lane Allen
James Lane Allen
James Oliver Curwood
James Oppenheim
James Otis
James R. Driscoll
Jane Abbott
Jane Austen
Jane L. Stewart
Janet Aldridge
Jens Peter Jacobsen
Jerome K. Jerome
Jessie Graham Flower
John Buchan
John Burroughs
John Cournos
John F. Kennedy
John Gay
John Glasworthy
John Habberton
John Joy Bell
John Kendrick Bangs
John Milton
John Philip Sousa
John Taintor Foote
Jonas Lauritz Idemil Lie
Jonathan Swift
Joseph A. Altsheler
Joseph Carey
Joseph Conrad
Joseph E. Badger Jr
Joseph Hergesheimer
Joseph Jacobs
Jules Vernes
Julian Hawthrone
Julie A Lippmann
Justin Huntly McCarthy
Kakuzo Okakura
Karle Wilson Baker
Kate Chopin
Kenneth Grahame
Kenneth McGaffey
Kate Langley Bosher
Kate Langley Bosher
Katherine Cecil Thurston
Katherine Stokes
L. A. Abbot
L. T. Meade

L. Frank Baum	Owen Johnson	Stephen Crane
Latta Griswold	P.G. Wodehouse	Stewart Edward White
Laura Dent Crane	Paul and Mabel Thorne	Stijn Streuvels
Laura Lee Hope	Paul G. Tomlinson	Swami Abhedananda
Laurence Housman	Paul Severing	Swami Parmananda
Lawrence Beasley	Percy Brebner	T. S. Ackland
Leo Tolstoy	Percy Keese Fitzhugh	T. S. Arthur
Leonid Andreyev	Peter B. Kyne	The Princess Der Ling
Lewis Carroll	Plato	Thomas A. Janvier
Lewis Sperry Chafer	Quincy Allen	Thomas A Kempis
Lilian Bell	R. Derby Holmes	Thomas Anderton
Lloyd Osbourne	R. L. Stevenson	Thomas Bailey Aldrich
Louis Hughes	R. S. Ball	Thomas Bulfinch
Louis Joseph Vance	Rabindranath Tagore	Thomas De Quincey
Louis Tracy	Rahul Alvares	Thomas Dixon
Louisa May Alcott	Ralph Bonehill	Thomas H. Huxley
Lucy Fitch Perkins	Ralph Henry Barbour	Thomas Hardy
Lucy Maud Montgomery	Ralph Victor	Thomas More
Luther Benson	Ralph Waldo Emmerson	Thornton W. Burgess
Lydia Miller Middleton	Rene Descartes	U. S. Grant
Lyndon Orr	Ray Cummings	Upton Sinclair
M. Corvus	Rex Beach	Valentine Williams
M. H. Adams	Rex E. Beach	Various Authors
Margaret E. Sangster	Richard Harding Davis	Vaughan Kester
Margret Howth	Richard Jefferies	Victor Appleton
Margaret Vandercook	Richard Le Gallienne	Victor G. Durham
Margaret W. Hungerford	Robert Barr	Victoria Cross
Margret Penrose	Robert Frost	Virginia Woolf
Maria Edgeworth	Robert Gordon Anderson	Wadsworth Camp
Maria Thompson Daviess	Robert L. Drake	Walter Camp
Mariano Azuela	Robert Lansing	Walter Scott
Marion Polk Angellotti	Robert Lynd	Washington Irving
Mark Overton	Robert Michael Ballantyne	Wilbur Lawton
Mark Twain	Robert W. Chambers	Wilkie Collins
Mary Austin	Rosa Nouchette Carey	Willa Cather
Mary Catherine Crowley	Rudyard Kipling	Willard F. Baker
Mary Cole	Saint Augustine	William Dean Howells
Mary Hastings Bradley	Samuel B. Allison	William le Queux
Mary Roberts Rinehart	Samuel Hopkins Adams	W. Makepeace Thackeray
Mary Rowlandson	Sarah Bernhardt	William W. Walter
M. Wollstonecraft Shelley	Sarah C. Hallowell	William Shakespeare
Maud Lindsay	Selma Lagerlof	Winston Churchill
Max Beerbohm	Sherwood Anderson	Yei Theodora Ozaki
Myra Kelly	Sigmund Freud	Yogi Ramacharaka
Nathaniel Hawthrone	Standish O'Grady	Young E. Allison
Nicolo Machiavelli	Stanley Weyman	Zane Grey
O. F. Walton	Stella Benson	
Oscar Wilde	Stella M. Francis	

Lightning Source LLC
Chambersburg PA
CBHW050035180626
46810CB00002B/727